CULVER CITY

Pictorial Research by Laura Cordova Molmud
"Partners in Progress" by Cynthia Simone

Produced in cooperation with the
Culver City Chamber of Commerce

Windsor Publications, Inc.
Chatsworth, California

CULVER CITY

The Heart of Screenland

An Illustrated History

by Julie Lugo Cerra

Windsor Publications, Inc.—History Book Division
Managing Editor: Karen Story
Design Director: Ellen Ifrah
Photo Director: Susan L. Wells
Executive Editor: Pamela Schroeder

Staff for *Culver City: The Heart of Screenland*
Manuscript Editor: Teri Davis Greenberg
Production Editor, Text: Mary Jo Scharf
Photo Editors: Loren Prostano and Larry Molmud
Senior Editor, Corporate Biographies: Jeffrey Reeves
Customer Service Manager: Phyllis Feldman-Schroeder
Editorial Assistants: Elizabeth Anderson, Alex Arredondo, Kate Coombs,
Lori Erbaugh, Wilma Huckabey
Publisher's Representative, Corporate Biographies: Irene Gresick
Designer: Christina L. Rosepapa
Layout Artist, Corporate Biographies: C. L. Murray
Layout Artist, Editorial: Bonnie Felt

Windsor Publications, Inc.
Elliot Martin, Chairman of the Board
James L. Fish III, Chief Operating Officer
Mac Buhler, Vice President/Sponsor Acquisitions

Library of Congress Cataloging-in-Publication Data:
Cerra, Julie Lugo, 1945-
Culver City : the heart of screenland / an illustrated history by Julie Lugo Cerra ;
pictorial research by Laura Cordova Molmud.
144 p.
Includes bibliographic references and index.
ISBN 0-89781-441-X
1. Culver City (Calif.)–History. 2. Culver City (Calif.)–Description–Views. 3. Culver
City (Calif.)–Industries. I. Simone, Cynthia. II. Title.
F869.C95C47 1992   91-28134
979.4'93—dc20   CIP

Contents

*Dedicated to Charles Reyes Lugo and
Mary Margaret Kleopfer Lugo, who gave me
a sense of history and purpose.*

Acknowledgments

La Ballona School students have much to smile about as school lets out for the summer, and their vacation begins. Photo by Amy Seidman-Tighe

THE TASK OF WRITING A HISTORY BOOK JUST REINFORCES ONE'S humility. Research must be broad in scope, and limits have to be established and honored, knowing that it could be so much better, more complete, "if I could just include this, too . . . " The City of Culver City, the Culver City Unified School District, and the people and organizations of Culver City have been so helpful, I just wish I could have used more to show them off.

It was such fun to look through the City Archives, and I cannot thank City Clerk Pauline Dolce enough for the opportunity to rummage through the original dusty minutes that brought those early beginnings of the city to life . . . like reading the very motion that gave the first city clerk an extra stipend to act as the janitor!

Newspapers provided local color, in the context of the times. I am grateful for all of the mornings Roy Donovan shared his Citizen Building office so that I could go through years of bound newspapers in the very building where the presses ran. And thanks to my favorite modern managing editor, John Hartmire of Coast Media, who provided access to microfilm files, so that I could complete my research and even read Helen Black's "Little Black Book" and some great ads for the flavor of the "olden days."

The Culver City Historical Society (especially co-presidents Linda Brady and Sam Cerra) provided access to their "closet," where I found an abundance of information and photos. I hope the society's collection will find its way into a community museum soon, where others can also enjoy seeing evidence of Culver City's beginnings, struggles, and accomplishments.

Josie Zoretich and the Culver City Library staff were always there to help, and I really appreciate their time and guidance. And the staff of the Southwest Museum was invaluable with their expertise.

There are always a few special people who are wonderful resources, like Pat Culver Battle, Gladys Chandler, Alene Houck Johnson, Syd Kronenthal, Carmen Shaw Simmons, Marc Wanamaker, Beverly Machado Szabo, and retired City Treasurer Lu Herrera.

Encouragement made this endeavor a real pleasure. I would like to thank Clarita Young, who pushed me down the "historical trail," and Steve Rose and the Chamber of Commerce, who believed in my capabilities. The Windsor Publications staff and their cheerful guidance made me breathe more than one sigh of relief. And to my delightful daughter, Michele, and husband Sam, a big hug for your patience with this often frazzled writer and the disarray of materials "up with which you had to put."

Happy 75th, Culver City . . . and many more!   Julie Lugo Cerra 1992

1 *Setting the Stage*

FLOWING THROUGH THE VALLEY THAT WOULD LATER BE CALLED La Ballona was a creek fed by *cienegas* (swamps) and lakes from the Hollywood Mountains to the Baldwin Hills. Willows, sycamores, and tules waved in the breeze along its rich silt banks. It was this, La Ballona Creek, along with a temperate climate and fertile ground, that encouraged settlement of the valley.

Shoshoneans were the first known inhabitants of the area that would later become Culver City. (Shoshonean refers to a linguistic branch, more specifically, Uto-Aztecan stock.) They were a peaceful people who lived in loosely organized tribelets, had a 3,500-word vocabulary, and even permitted females to become chiefs and shamans.

Because of their proximity to the San Gabriel Mission, these people were later known as Gabrielinos. Their housing consisted of dome-shaped huts framed in willow and thatched with tule or grass. A hole in the roof allowed smoke to escape. These huts, called *jacals* or *wicki-ups*, were used for sleeping as well as protection from the elements. La Ballona Valley offered water, safety, and an abundance of food. Small game—rats, gophers, and rabbits—was plentiful, while vegetation growing along the creek and hillsides provided edible berries, seeds, and roots.

These early inhabitants of Southern California are considered to have been the most skillful basketmakers among primitive peoples, and had a monetary system in place before the Spaniards arrived. Southern California Indians were also the only ones in the continental United States using board boats at the time the Europeans came to North America. The boards were lashed and bound together with asphalt found in the area of the La Brea Tar Pits. Measuring 20 to 25 feet in length, Gabrielino vessels were used for fishing, trading, and transportation.

The Gabrielinos practiced a monotheistic religion and believed in an afterlife. Their most important ceremonies honored the dead, and the males were generally responsible for rituals and sacred rites. The chief was charged with administration—giving direction, admonishing poor behavior, storing and redistributing economic resources—and, with the aid of a council, was the final authority on tribal matters. He was also recognized as the high priest with possession of the "sacred bundle," the link between the sacred past and the present.

Able-bodied men hunted, fished, and assisted with some plant gathering. Bows and arrows were used for big game, and harpoons, spears, and clubs were used to catch sea animals. Older men made the political decisions, taught skills, and crafted hunting and ceremonial equipment. Women gathered plants, prepared food, and produced baskets, pots, and clothing. They also performed supplemental dancing and singing for rituals. Children were cared for by the older women and unmarried girls.

Parents selected their children's spouses; the perfect husband was considered one who fulfilled his obligations and was skilled in economic pursuits or possessed religious knowl-

edge. For a young woman to be chosen as a wife, she was expected to be hardworking, produce food, be able to bear children, and get along with her in-laws. When a marriage was arranged, the families bestowed gifts upon one another, with the wife's family receiving the larger endowment. The birth of a child signified a binding of two families, both economically and socially.

Young married couples lived with the husband's family. Though divorce was possible, it was considered a serious step, and the marriage gifts had to be returned. The wife was usually blamed for the divorce, with valid reasons including her inability to bear children, her infidelity, or her poor behavior. In the case of an unfaithful wife, a husband could choose to claim the spouse of his wife's lover.

The Gabrielinos were one of only of a few Native American cultures in which cross-cultural marriages were allowed. This resulted in connecting them with the Luiseño, Cahuilla, and Tipai-Ipai tribes.

The Gabrielinos used mortars and pestles for grinding, baskets for sifting flour, and hot rocks for cooking. They cooked porridges, breads, and tortillas in clay vessels, and baked, boiled, broiled, and poached fresh meat in baskets or pots in pits or over an open fire.

BELOW: Gabrielino women are seen here grinding corn-meal, weaving baskets, and going about daily chores in a typical village setting. Courtesy, San Fernando Valley Historical Society

RIGHT: Because of the mild climate and abundance of land, the Gabrielinos were able to spend a significant portion of their daily lives pursuing artistic, cultural, and spiritual endeavors. Courtesy, First American Title Insurance Company

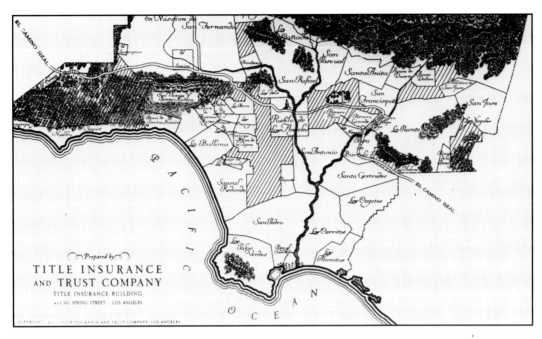

The boundaries delineating Rancho La Ballona appear near the center of this map labeled "The Old Spanish and Mexican Ranchos of Los Angeles County." Prepared by Los angeles' Title Insurance and Trust Company in 1912, the map depicts the area as it appeared in the mid-1800s. Courtesy, California Historical Society

Pots were sealed to preserve food from one season to another, and large, woven granaries stored acorns and other reserves. Meat was dried in the sun for future use.

In warm or hot weather, Gabrielino men went naked or wore hide loin cloths. In cool weather they donned buckskin shirts, jackets, and short trousers. Waistcords were used to carry objects. The women wore knee-length skirts made of grasses, bark, or skins. To protect their heads while carrying fishnets, round basket caps were worn. Children rarely wore any clothing. In the winter, however, the entire family would put on animal-skin robes, or sometimes robes made of birdskins with the feathers intact.

Ritual costumes for chiefs and shamans were colorfully designed with plumage, fur, shells, and beads, and a headdress was sometimes worn. Bone, abalone shell, and steatite (soapstone) beads were used as ornaments, while necklaces, bracelets, and anklets were made of shells, beads, or human hair. Women decorated their bodies for rituals with red ochre and paints made from charcoal and white clay. Tattooing was common, facilitated by thorns or flint slivers and dye made from vegetables or charcoal. While girls were tattooed on their chins and foreheads

Franciscan missionary Junipero Serra founded Mission San Gabriel during his years of tireless and devoted work for the church. Courtesy, Bancroft Library

before puberty, adult women could use this form of marking from around their eyes down to their breasts. Some men tattooed their foreheads with vertical and horizontal lines.

The Gabrielino culture changed dramatically with the establishment of Mission San Gabriel in 1771, as the Spanish mission fathers converted and exerted control over these people.

The Machado hacienda, pictured here, housed one of the most prominent families in the Culver City area. The home was built in 1828 below the hills near El Rincon School and La Ballona Creek. It was later destroyed by a flood. Courtesy, Seaver Center for Western History Research, Natural History Museum of Los Angeles County

Jose Sepulveda, owner of Rancho San Vicente y Santa Monica, represented one of the four families whose ranchos bordered Rancho La Ballona. Courtesy, Seaver Center for Western History Research, Natural History Museum of Los Angeles County

About 10 years after the establishment of Mission San Gabriel, Jose Manuel Machado y Yanez, along with Alferez Cayetano Limon, arrived at the mission. The men were part of a volunteer contingent sent by the governor of California to guard the Santa Barbara presidio. Approximately two months later, on September 4, 1781, a procession led by California Governor Felipe de Neve y Perea marched nine miles across the valley to the Rio de la Porciuncula to establish the Pueblo de la Nuestra Senora la Reina de los Angeles. Meanwhile, Machado and others were permitted to stay at San Gabriel until spring. In the fall Machado's wife, Maria de la Luz Valenzuela y Avilas, whom he had married before leaving on his trek, gave birth to their first son, Jose Manuel, who was baptized at the San Gabriel Mission in November.

On March 26, 1782, Machado and his small family began the journey up El Camino Real with Padre Pedro Cambon and Padre Junipero Serra. On March 31, Father Serra dedicated Mission San Buenaventura, continuing up to the Royal Presidio of Santa Barbara, where the Machados stayed for two years. In 1786 Machado was stationed at San Buenaventura. He moved back to Santa Barbara in 1788, and then transferred to La Purisima Concepcion. Eventually, Jose Manuel

and Maria Machado retired to the pueblo of Los Angeles, where their last child was born in 1799. By 1790, the original 11 families in the pueblo had increased to 28, and when the Machados returned in 1797, there were 70 families and a population of 315. Jose Manuel Machado remained in the pueblo until his death in 1810. He was survived by his wife and eight of his nine children.

As early as the mid-1780s the residents of the pueblo began to use outlying areas for cattle grazing. In 1819 Jose Manuel Machado's fifth son, Jose Agustín, and Felipe de Jesus Talamantes received a permit to graze their cattle on the land known as Rancho del los Quintos. Maintaining that the permit was invalid and that the land belonged to the town, the *regidores* (officials) and 30 of the pueblo's citizens filed a complaint. When Acting Comandante Moraga refused to make a definite judgment, Machado and Talamantes looked west. Of particular interest was the small valley bounded by the Baldwin Hills on the south, the Cheviot Hills on the north, and extending toward Playa del Rey. Swampy tidelands were scattered throughout, with an abundance of wild game. Because no surveyors were available, permits were generally issued based on the number of cattle to graze. Machado and Talamantes family tradition fur-

ther defined the land held as that which one could circle on horseback from sunrise to sunset. Agustin Machado is said to have practiced for weeks on his horse, one of the fastest in the pueblo. He camped at the foot of the del Rey hills and when dawn broke, began the ride that would outline Rancho La Ballona. (The origin of the word Ballona is still in question. Some hypothesize that it is a misspelling of *ballena*, meaning whale, since it was said that at the west end of the creek one could spot whales. Others have postulated that it sounded like the pronunciation of a coastal town in Spain, the home of some of the area's early settlers.)

And so, in 1820, Agustin Machado, his younger brother Ygnacio, Felipe Talamantes, and his oldest son, Tomas, received a permit to graze cattle on their 14,000-acre rancho. The Machados and Talamantes families, with the help of Jose Manuel Cota, a Machado brother-in-law, worked Rancho La Ballona with the help of Gabrielinos. Their fertile land yielded corn, pumpkins, beans, and wheat. Vineyards and fruit trees thrived along the creek, and the hills were dotted with sheep, while herds of cattle and horses grazed on the rich pasturelands.

Spanish rule of California came to an end in 1822, and Mexican rule began. In 1828 the Mexican government issued a *reglamento* that outlined the procedure for granting land. Few Californians, including the owners of Rancho La Ballona, applied at that time. Yet in 1833, when Governor Jose Figueroa issued a proclamation secularizing the missions, the granting

Ranchers and farmers erected the valley's first school, La Ballona School, which was attended by students from a district bounded by La Cienega Boulevard to the ocean and from Redondo Beach north to the Santa Monica Mountains. Reportedly, the teacher received $50 a month to instruct 160 children. Courtesy, Julie Lugo Cerra

of land began with vigor. Finally, in 1839, the Machado and Talamantes families took steps to acquire Ballona. They were granted legal title to the rancho in November of that year by Governor Alvarado. Conditions included that a house must be built on the land, that it must be lived in by the grantee, and that a survey had to be done.

Rancho La Ballona was bounded on the east by Policarpio Higuera's Rancho Rincon de los Bueyes, on the north by Señor Alanis' San Jose de Buenos Ayres, on the west by Antonio Ignacio Avila's Sausal Redondo, and on the south by Señor Jose Sepulveda's San Vicente y Santa Monica. The survey was conducted by Manuel Dominguez, Second Justice of the Peace ad Interim. He arrived at La Ballona, notified the surrounding landowners, and despite objections by Avila and Sepulveda, since they could not document their concerns, the *diseño* stood. A period of prosperity and few problems followed for Rancho La Ballona.

In 1824 Agustin Machado married 18-year-old Maria Petra Manuela Buelna y Mejias, whose mother came to the area in the same expedition as Agustin's parents. Maria died

giving birth to their first son, Juan Bautista, in June 1826. The following January, Agustin married Maria Ramona Sepulveda y Serrano. Her family owned Rancho San Vicente y Santa Monica, which bordered Rancho La Ballona. Fourteen children were born of that marriage. In 1826 Agustin's brother Ygnacio married Maria Estefania Palomares y Saenz. Within two years they settled on nearby Canada del Centinela. Felipe and Tomas Talamantes and their families moved to adjacent Rancho Rincon de los Bueyes.

Agustin Machado was in complete charge of Rancho La Ballona in 1834. The adobe he had built for his first wife near Sawtelle and Overland was washed away in heavy rains. Machado's second adobe was built on higher ground, at Overland and Jefferson.

Life in the pueblo and on the ranchos was primitive in the early days, but California's economic isolation was lessened as more ships anchored in San Pedro Bay. Don Agustin Machado took an active part in coastal trade as Rancho La Ballona prospered. He followed ox-drawn *carretas* (carts) to San Pedro, where he traded tallow, beaver skins, dried beef and beans, peas and lentils for necessities, and luxuries from New England traders and those from the Orient. Machado had expanded his land holdings to the pueblo, where he cultivated grapes and fruit trees, with additional property in Rancho Santa Rosa, in San Diego, and holdings in adjacent La Laguna Rancho. He became famous for his white wine, farming, and horse trading. Machado was a prominent citizen and active politically. He served as *juez del campo*, "judge of the plains," in 1838 and 1848, enforcing the law, and in 1856, he held the title of justice of the peace.

The Gold Rush had brought thousands of newcomers to California, some seeking gold, others looking for land. In Washington, D.C., it became apparent that a land policy needed to be established. So the year after California became a state, the Land Act of March 3, 1851 (legislation also known as the "Gwin Bill"), established a three-person Board of Land Commissioners in San Francisco to decide upon the validity of California land titles. Petition was made and granted to hold hearings in Los Angeles, since the Northern California location was a financial burden to residents in Southern California. In 1852 Agustin Machado filed formal petition with the Board of Land Commissioners, and in February 1854 Commissioner Thomas Camp-

bell handed down an opinion in his favor, which took until January 1856 to be confirmed by a district court. By the time Agustin Machado died at the age of 70 in 1865, he had held title to his land under three governments. With the boundary disputes that ensued, it became the work of Machado heirs to clear the title to their land. It was not until December 8, 1873, that the land office issued

LEFT and BELOW: With the onset of the Gold Rush and the subsequent population explosion, many cattle ranchers prospered as the demand for beef increased. Courtesy, Seaver Center for Western History Research, Natural History Museum of Los Angeles County

Seating 200 parishioners, St. Augustine's Church was one of the first churches to be built in Culver City. Until it was completed in 1887, churchgoers had to travel to St. Monica's Church for religious services. Photo by Amy Seidman-Tighe

used to secure the loan, precipitated the eventual division of Rancho La Ballona. At the end of the six-month loan period, Talamantes could not pay the $2,353.26 owing plus an additional $238.81 in costs. He lost his property when the case went to court, and on December 31, 1855, at public auction, Wilson paid $2,000 as the highest bidder for one-quarter ownership in La Ballona. The new owner's title was established in 1859. Wilson then sold his 3,480-acre share of the rancho for $4,500 to John Sanford, James T. Young, and Young's son, John D.

James T. Young purchased a small adobe and moved onto the rancho. Before Felipe Talamantes died in 1856, his quarter interest was deeded to his three children. Only Tomás was living at the time of his father's death, so his grandchildren received their parents' portions. Within the next 10 years, Felipe's quarter was owned by nine people; John Sanford deeded his share to his young nephew, George Addision Sanford; and James T. Young sold 50 acres to Willis Prather. When Agustin Machado died in 1865, his interest was divided among his wife and 13 living children, and within a month of Machado's death, John D. Young filed the required petition in court to partition the rancho. Before it was settled, the elder Young died, leaving his portion to his wife, Elenda, and son, John. John sold this portion to Addison Rose for $15. By 1867 Ygnacio Machado sold a small part of his quarter to Dolores Aguilar y Yorba and deeded the remainder to his four sons. When the district court handed down the interlocutory decree in November 1867, the owners of Rancho La Ballona numbered 32.

During the Civil War an army base called Camp Latham was established on La Ballona Creek, near Jefferson. The camp served as headquarters for the 1st California Infantry Volunteers; its purpose was to keep perceived Southern sympathy in check. Camp Latham was abandoned in 1862, when a new base was built in San Pedro.

As the old Rancho La Ballona and those

the patent giving clear title under U.S. law to a deceased Agustin Machado and his partners.

The Yankees who came to California during the Gold Rush introduced lending practices with high monthly interest rates, resulting in repayment double or triple the amount of the original loan. One Californian caught in just such a financial disaster was Tomás Talamantes. He borrowed $1,500 in June 1854 from two Americans, Benjamin D. Wilson and William Sanford. This six-month loan at five percent per month, with one quarter of the undivided interest in Ballona

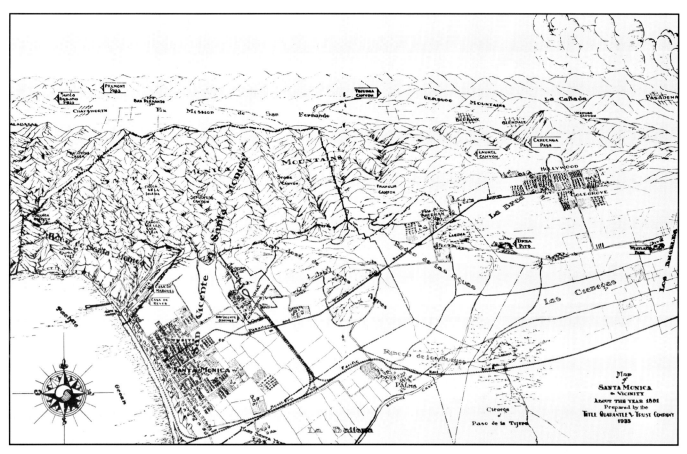

adjacent were divided, families increased, and in 1865-1866 La Ballona School celebrated its first year. It was one of the oldest schools in the county and a part of the Ballona School District. According to records in the California State Archives, a Miss Craft from Boston was the teacher. The school year lasted seven months, and the teacher's monthly salary was $50, including board. The average daily attendance was 19 pupils. The original wooden-frame schoolhouse, located at Washington Boulevard and Elenda Street, was rebuilt after the turn of the century on the same site.

Before 1900 there were few structures in the area, and most were residential. The Saenz Dry Goods Store stood at the corner of Overland and Washington, with the Machado Post Office located inside the store. The Halfway House, famous for wines and pickles, was located on Washington Boulevard, halfway between Los Angeles and the beach. (The Beacon Laundry occupies that site today.)

In 1883 J. Francisco Figueroa donated land fronting a dirt Washington Boulevard for a church. Until St. Augustine's Church was completed in 1887, local parishioners traveled to the Old Soldier's Home on Sawtelle or to St. Monica's for religious services. Priests traveled from St. Monica's to say Mass at the new, 200-seat chapel.

A marker placed in Carlson Park in 1963 by the Chamber of Commerce names the first seven families in the area: Machado, Talamantes, Higuera, Ybarra, Lugo, Rocha, and Saenz. Judging from early maps, the only omission might be the Cotas.

As the twentieth century approached, the ranchos saw further division, and the arrival of the railroads yielded a marked increase in the population of Los Angeles, an increase that would directly affect the development of La Ballona Valley.

This 1881 map depicts Santa Monica and its surrounding area. Some of the sites on the map are significant to the history of Culver City: La Ballona, La Ballona Creek, Rincon de los Bueyes, Palms, and Rancho San Vicente y Santa Monica. Courtesy, Seaver Center for Western History Research, Natural History Museum of Los Angeles County

2 *Lights, Camera, Action*

CULVER CITY WAS JUST WAITING IN THE WINGS TO BECOME A REALITY. The pueblo of Los Angeles had experienced steady growth since its beginning in 1781, and by 1850, when California was admitted to the Union, Los Angeles had grown from 11 families to nearly 2,000 residents. The numbers continued to spiral, and by the turn of the century the area boasted a population of 102,479. Climate, transportation, publicity, and the development of aqueducts to bring water from the interior regions of the state all contributed to the region's spectacular growth.

Southern California's mild climate was desirable, as was its scenic countryside. The contrast of the mountains, deserts, and beaches nearby was startling to the easterner.

The state's isolation came to an end when the first transcontinental railroad route celebrated completion in 1869. The gold spike was driven at Promontory Pointe, Utah, just a century after the Spaniards completed California's first mission. The Central Pacific, formed by the "Big Four," Collis P. Huntington, Charles Crocker, Mark Hopkins, and Leland Stanford, could carry a passenger from New York to San Francisco in seven days. Before the advent of the railroad, a covered wagon took six months to travel from Missouri to the Pacific Coast. Despite references to Los Angeles as the "Queen of the Cow Counties" by flip San Franciscans, Angelinos voted in 1872 to subsidize the railroad to come to L.A. Los Angeles and San Francisco were connected by train in 1876, and the arrival of the Atchison, Topeka & Santa Fe in 1886 offered a second transcontinental link. With migration came another land boom. One rate war in the mid-1880s brought prices of a ticket from St. Louis to Los Angeles down to one dollar. (This ticket price only lasted 15 minutes!)

Short-line railroads begun by real estate developers were soon taken over by the transcontinental railroads. During that same period, Judge Robert Maclay Widney, who established the first real estate office in Los Angeles and was one of the founders of the University of Southern California, built the first streetcar line. His single track opened in 1874, a 2.5-mile run down Main, from Mission Plaza to 6th Street. The cost was 10 cents a ride! The interurban trolleys, which were eventually replaced by the automobile, contributed to the horizontal development of the Los Angeles area. The population spread into remote regions, forming suburbs. The Pacific Electric was the largest interurban system in the United States, and Culver City was founded at a junction point.

Silent-film actress Theda Bara, one of the pioneers of the movie industry, strikes a coquettish pose. Courtesy, Culver City Historical Society

The Palms was a triangular subdivision established in December 1886. Ballona Boulevard (now Washington), First Street (now Overland), and Manning Avenue were its boundaries. Joseph Curtis, E.H. Sweetser, and C.J. Harrison paid $40,000 for these 500 acres, part of the Macedonio Aguilar allotment of Rancho La Ballona. Few structures broke up the landscape. The Halfway House, famous for its wines and pickled olives, was located on Washington Boulevard halfway between L.A. and Santa Monica, just west of Francisco Higuera's adobe. The Saenz family dry-goods store was farther west on Washington, at Overland. The Machado Post Office, the first in what later became Culver City, was located inside.

Moye L. Wicks outlined the idea of a much-needed harbor at "Port Ballona" in the mid-1880s. There was other competition for L.A.'s harbor, and finally, by the turn of the century, construction of a deep-water harbor at Long Beach-San Pedro was endorsed by Congress. In 1902 Port Ballona became Playa del Rey.

In 1904 Abbot Kinney bought acres of tide flats and lagoons south of Ocean Park. Here he created "Venice in America," a variation of its Italian namesake, with canals for streets, an amusement pier with food and games, and a ballroom and ship cafe which drew enormous crowds on the weekends. Hotels sprang up, and the resort became a favorite destination of Red Car passengers.

Camillo Cereghino and his San Francisco/ Oakland associates formed the Washington Boulevard Improvement Company to purchase the remaining 150 acres of Macedonio Aguilar's pasturelands in 1912. This land, laid out the way it remains today, was located from Washington Boulevard to La Ballona Creek and was known as Washington Park or Tract 1775. Cereghino kept a piece of land for his own home, a structure that still sits behind high fences amid orchards, on the corner of Madison Avenue and Farragut Drive.

The streets were named for U.S. presidents and other people of prominence.

In 1910 a 30-year-old Nebraskan named Harry H. Culver went to work for realtor I.N. Van Nuys, learning the ropes of L.A. real estate. After studying the Los Angeles area, Culver targeted for development land halfway between Los Angeles and the sea. (His daughter, Pat Culver Battle, remembers hearing how he even conducted a year-long analysis of the area's temperature.) On July 25, 1913, at the California Club in Los Angeles, Harry Culver, of the newly formed Culver Investment Company, announced his plans for a city that would be a balanced residential/commercial community.

Culver's new company began by acquiring blocks in Palms and adjacent acreage, northwest of Washington Boulevard. P.H. Albright, a civil engineer, was employed to subdivide the heart of the city. Harry Culver's office was the first building, built in 1913 and located on what was recorded as Main Street. Original officers of the Culver Investment Company were President Harry Culver, Treasurer Lawrence M. Welsh, and Directors R.P. Sherman, Delphin Delmas, and H.C. Nutt. In the October 31, 1914, edition of the *Culver City Call,* a quote from one local real estate critic read: "[Culver City] was the greatest piece of real estate impertinence ever foisted on an unsuspecting public."

Within a year of its formation, Culver City had a grocery store, plumbing and hardware shop, macaroni factory, bank, candy store, newspaper (the *Culver City Call*), homes, and a real estate sales force of 150. Trees were planted, a lighting system designed, and streets paved.

Harry H. Culver became world renowned as an innovative promoter. He bused in families to see property and awarded a lot to the winner of a prettiest-baby contest. He instituted a marathon race from Los Angeles to Culver City, held parades of decorated cars led by a band, sponsored a "polo game" with Fords, and had a searchlight placed on top of his office. One newspaper ad read: "Wise men of the East followed a star, Wise men of the West follow the searchlight to Culver City." A pharmacist from Palms won a trip around the world for naming "Media Park."

Gladys Gale E. Kotsvasz recalls her mother telling a story about plans she had with her sister for lunch. It seems these two enterprising and thrifty young women saw a bus advertising a ride to Culver City and a free lunch. They took advantage of the offer and were so

In 1916 a bond issue was granted for $55,000 to build the Culver City Grammar School, now Linwood Howe School. It was the beginning of a school system that would become known for its academic excellence. Courtesy, Culver City Historical Society

Harry Culver, Father of Culver City

HOW I KNEW MY FATHER
"My Tribute" by Pat Culver Battle

Hard-working; healthy
Active; affectionate
Reliable; respectable
Reasonable; realistic
Yearning for progress; youthful

Humorous; happy

Creative; capable
Unexpected; unforgettable
Loving; loyally patriotic
Vigorous; vital
Energetic; encouraging me
Responsible; responsive to my
young thoughts + dreams
(11-9-83)

The Culvers were descended from Edward Colver, who arrived in Massachusetts from England in 1635. Harry Hazel Culver was born January 22, 1880, in Milford, Nebraska. He was the middle child of five. Harry, his three brothers, and his sister were raised on the family farm, where they learned the work ethic from their strict disciplinarian father. Following in his National Guard brigadier general father's footsteps, Harry enlisted during the Spanish-American War. He was underage, but managed to serve as trumpeter, working his way up to sergeant. Harry attended

Doane College, a prep school, and then went off to the University of Nebraska for three years, where he was a member of Alpha Tau Omega fraternity. Culver's entrepreneurial skills enabled him to finance his education by performing a variety of jobs, including taking in laundry. He and his father started their own bottled spring-water business at one point; their only mistake was not keeping the controlling stock.

In 1901 Harry Culver left for the Philippines, where he went into the mercantile business in Olongapa, then served as a reporter on the *Manila Times*. He was also assigned as a special agent in the customs department. After three and a half years, he returned stateside and was assigned to customs special duty in St. Louis and Detroit. In 1910 Culver resigned this post to move to California.

After he arrived in Southern California, Harry H. Culver went to work for Mr. I.N. Van Nuys in the real estate business for a year. Van Nuys offered to make him a manager, but Culver did not stay. He wanted to venture out on his own. After intense study, Harry Culver pinpointed the area he wanted to develop. He announced his plans in 1913 at a California Club luncheon in downtown Los Angeles. After the formation of

the Culver Investment Company, Harry located his office on Main Street of the city that would later carry his name. He stood on the banks of La Ballona Creek, watching Thomas Ince shoot a movie with Indians in canoes "on location." Culver was able to sell Ince property on Washington Boulevard, which was the beginning of the "Heart of Screenland." Culver's daughter, Pat, claims that her father was "not really a super salesman—he knew what people needed!" He was a master of supply and demand.

It was during this period that Culver was driving along in his white Pierce Arrow, when a young woman caught his eye. She was wearing a yellow suit, and her rich brown hair was crowned with a spring straw hat. The 19-year-old actress was waiting for the Venice Short Line to go downtown. Her name was Lillian Roberts, and she was being groomed by Thomas Ince. She played "Emma," the second lead in *Rebecca*. Culver was considered too old for her, but he still managed to meet Miss Roberts and they eventually married, in June 1916. Their only child, Patricia, was born in August 1917, just a month before Culver City was incorporated.

Culver built a home for his family on Delmas Terrace, which was moved to Cheviot Hills, where

Courtesy, Culver City Historical Society

it still stands on Club Drive. The Culvers lived in this home for a year, as their 18-room mansion was constructed in clear view. Culver's daughter, admittedly biased, called her father "a fabulous rider, swimmer and ice hockey player." He also played tennis and owned his own ice hockey team at one time. Culver taught his daughter to ride, English style, at the Pacific Military Academy, which he founded as a tribute to his own father. She remembers having double reins and that she had to "hold all four in one little hand," keeping her right hand free for a sabre!

Culver was active in his town's politics and served on its Board of Trustees early on. He helped organize the Culver City Commercial & Savings Bank, Pacific Building and Loan Association, Pacific Military Academy, and the California Country Club, and built the Hunt Hotel, now known as the landmark Culver Hotel. He was also proud that he spawned University City. He flew his own plane and was known throughout the country for his expertise in real estate. He served as president of the California Real Estate Association as well as the National Association of Real Estate Boards.

Harry Culver donated 100 acres of land on which to build Loyola University, where he received an honorary Doctor of Laws in 1930. Culver survived the Great Depression, but met his own financial disaster later. He worked for the Los Angeles Chamber of Commerce for $1,000 a month, successfully recovering bonds. He liquidated his holdings and put his money in a Beverly Hills bank, where he lost all of it. He also helped raise funds for the near-bankrupt Harding College and worked to save San Francisco's Fremont Hotel.

In 1937, during a speaking tour, Culver sustained serious injuries to his leg when his car was hit head on. After the doctor ordered rest, Culver bought a house in Newport, where he enjoyed his 28-foot boat. Harry H. Culver died in August 1946 in a Hollywood hospital after suffering a number of strokes. His remains are in the mausoleum at Inglewood Park Cemetery.

Perhaps better than a eulogy and still pertinent is the foreword written by Laura McNeir Loud for *A Resume Of Culver City, California,* an illustrated publication compiled for the Culver City Woman's Club in 1922:

"A barley field, though beautiful in its changing verdure and waving grain, may hold little inspiration for the romanticist, but one practical, observant and far-seeing business man in his daily routine of duty through a certain stretch of growing barley, caught a vision full of such possibilities that the inspiration thus given led to immediate action."

The vision is still unfolding into realities seen in the continued growth and advancement of Culver City, California.

pleased with the area that the sisters also became neighbors on Duquesne Avenue. In nearby Venice the Neptune Theater advertised Society Night as a kickoff for a week-long turkey trot. The winner received a $100 certificate toward a lot in Culver City.

As Harry Culver's plans for development were moving forward, he witnessed the filming of a movie in 1915 at La Ballona Creek. Thomas Ince was shooting a Western "on location." The scene was complete with costumed Indians sporting painted faces as they rowed down a mighty "river." Harry Culver was hooked! His fascination with the movie industry helped him convince Thomas Ince to move from his Inceville studio north of Santa Monica to prime property on Washington Boulevard. This was to be the first of

Culver City's three major motion picture studios, which would provide for its sound economic base.

A $55,000 bond issue was passed in 1916 to build Culver Grammar School, which became part of the La Ballona School District. It was not until 1920, however, that the Los Angeles County Board of Supervisors changed the name to the Culver City School District. For a time Culver City had a school district without a school!

Annexing Culver City was a Los Angeles goal, but only the residents of Palms voted to become a part of the big city. On August 13, 1917, the Los Angeles County Board of Supervisors ordered an election to be held on September 8 for Culver City's incorporation. The new city elected a board of trustees: R.P.

LEFT: The first police and fire department station was located on Van Buren. Members from both departments posed for this photo in the 1920s. Courtesy, Culver City Historical Society

BELOW: With a dramatic increase in population, police protection became a most important necessity. Pictured here is the Culver City Police Department. Courtesy, Culver City Historical Society

Davidson, Dan F. Coombs, Walter Edwards, V.R. Day, and B.J. Higuera. Charles E. Shillito was elected city clerk and Harry Culver lost the election to C.N. Rosenthal for city treasurer. The townspeople held an all-day celebration in the streets of Culver City on September 15. Festivities began with a parade in the morning, baseball, sideshows, booths staffed by pretty girls, fireworks in the evening, and a Grand Ball in the clubhouse. The Board of Supervisors filed Culver City's articles of incorporation with the Secretary of State on September 20, 1917. It was official. Harry Culver's dream had begun to come true, with 1.2 square miles and the potential for growth.

The city fathers convened a preliminary meeting at the Culver City Club House on October 1. The Board of Trustees elected R.P. Davidson as their chairman. Davidson had been coaxed by Culver into starting the city's first hardware store; some 10 years later he would be the contractor for the city hall

on Culver Boulevard. He became a resident and businessman with only $400 in his pocket. Harry Culver attended the meeting, addressed the trustees, and city business began. The first resolution, adopted that evening, was to create the office of the city attorney, setting his salary at $50 per month. Ordinance No. 1 was also read, fixing the time and place of meetings of the board of trustees. Another resolution adopted by trustees provided for leasing, at $15 per month, the second floor of the theater on Main and Washington for city offices.

The challenges were just beginning for the new city. Within a few months, the city attorney changed three times. A city marshal was appointed to conduct the legal business of the city, and a committee of three contracted for police protection from the Los Angeles County Sheriff's Department. Resolution No. 15 provided for the appointment of temporary police officers. From 1918 to 1926 six marshals were appointed. Only one served longer than 10 months. In 1926 the average tenure of a police officer was less than two years. From 1926 through 1990 there would be 19 chiefs heading the police department.

To conserve energy, the trustees followed the example of other government agencies by discontinuing use of the illuminated sign over the city hall until "general conditions of the county improved." In March the entire city became one voting precinct; and four election officers—an inspector, judge, and two clerks—would be compensated at $4 each for the April election. The city offices became a polling place. B.J. Higuera and V.R. Day were elected to four-year terms, while Walter Edwards, Clyde W. Slater, and Dan F. Coombs assumed two-year terms. Katherine Megary defeated Charles E. Shillito for city clerk, and C.N. Rosenthal was elected city

RIGHT: Five years after moving to Culver City in 1913, Dan Coombs became mayor of the newly incorporated city. He was responsible for building business blocks and homes for many of its residents. Courtesy, Ronald H. Coombs

BELOW: Mayor Reve Houck was the city's leader when the movie industry was producing blockbuster hits. Pictured with Houck is movie genius Cecil B. deMille. Courtesy, Alene Houck Johnson

treasurer. Of the 79 ballots cast, 5 were rejected. (The small number of votes is a reminder that women did not have the right to vote until the 19th Amendment was ratified in 1920. In fact, Katherine Megary could not even vote for herself!) In May a night policeman was hired at $125 per month, and the city marshal became the ex officio tax and license collector. R.P. Davidson became the first building, plumbing, and city electrical inspector. The inspector's salary was set at $25 per month, only to be changed within the year to 75 percent of the permit fees he collected. The city treasurer's salary was established in June 1918 at $10 monthly. The first city health officer, Dr. W.S. Mortensen,

was appointed in August at $25 per month. Dr. Foster Hull was his successor. Dr. Hull built the first hospital in Culver City (later named as Historic Site No. 2 by the Culver City Historical Society). The lower front was Sunset Drugs, where Clarita Young worked at the "fountain."

In February 1919 Harry H. Culver was appointed as a trustee to fill the seat of Clyde W. Slater, who had resigned. Paul R. Cowles was hired as the first city engineer that same month. In March the trustees adopted an official map, defining the city's streets, roads, avenues, highways, and alleys.

Manuel "Sy" Saenz was appointed chief of the fire department in 1919, and the truck was stored in his garage. The entire fire department was volunteer at the time. The pay was one dollar for false alarms and four dollars for a real fire, whether the firemen worked 20 minutes or 16 hours. As the old-timers tell it, a fire caused real havoc, starting with the feat of moving the fire truck out of Saenz' Garage at Washington and what is

now Ince. Structures often burned to the ground before the firemen arrived. The truck was stored later at Earl Bobier's. L.B. Minnick, the fire chief for Ince Studios, helped as well, but the volunteer chief concept only lasted until the "boys" botched a fire at Mayor Clyde Slater's. In 1922 the trustees, with a little push from Slater, decided to hire a permanent chief. Fire Chief Frank Wilcox earned $175 a month in 1923.

In 1919 the board empowered the president to enter into a contract with the Auto Club of Southern California to install traffic signs posting speed limits. Just before Christmas, action was taken to appoint Katherine Megary, still the city clerk, as janitor for $25 a month. By early 1920 the city engineer's plan of numbering houses was adopted. In the April 12, 1920, election, 37 votes were cast, and three trustees were elected: Daniel Coombs, Harry H. Culver, and Clyde W. Slater. Katherine Megary ran unopposed for city clerk, and Charles E. Shillito received the highest number of votes for city treasurer. In

This view of Culver City in 1920 shows the studios in the distance, and Baldwin Hills in the background. Courtesy, Alene Houck Johnson

RIGHT: Built by Harry Culver in 1924 and known then as the Hunt Hotel, the six-story building is located at the intersection of Washington and Culver boulevards and is now known as the Culver Hotel. This is a modern look at the historic site. Courtesy, Julie Lugo Cerra

BELOW: The Steller Bros. Hardware store on Main Street has been in business since 1923. Courtesy, Culver City Historical Society

1921 there was a special election for the "Smith Annexation," which was the first of the 37 to date.

Harry Culver established the Pacific Military Academy in 1922 in memory of his father, the late General J.H. Culver, U.S. Army Volunteers. The academy was moved in 1925 from Washington Boulevard to its permanent location near Cardiff and Cattaraugus, just north of the city. The cost for boarding students was $800 a year, while the annual rate for day school was $200.

With business flourishing, the Culver City Chamber of Commerce emerged in 1921. At the foot of Main Street was Van Dusen's, the city's first pharmacy, and the 1st National Bank of Culver City. On the street itself were the city offices above the Meralta Theatre, the Adams Hotel, Bert's Toggery, California Bakery, a post office, Steller Bros. and Skoog Hardware, a restaurant, Carlin's Drug Store, and Culver's two real estate offices. The hub of business activity, Main Street had a planted median with a flagpole in the center. (The flagpole was later moved to Culver Grammar School.) By the end of the decade, the Bank of Italy would have its grand opening and the Chamber of Commerce would have moved into its offices on Washington Boulevard. The city worked well with the chamber, and, in 1927, $100 was donated from the "Music and Promotion Fund" to assist in the completion of a booklet advertising Culver City.

The 1920s saw a burgeoning of the downtown area. The Washington Building, also known as the Flat Iron Building, was built; some of its office space was used for a post office and a bookstore. Today, the Washington Building is listed on the National Register of Historic Places. Harry Culver moved his home from Washington and Delmas Terrace to Cheviot Hills so he could supervise the construction of his mansion. Culver City was to have seven miles of Washington Boulevard within its boundaries, with King's Famous Tropical Inn serving chicken dinners (from the 1920s to the 1960s) at Adams. The Yellow Cab Company was located at the east end. Among the other Washington Boulevard commercial residents were a number of car dealers, Dr. Foster Hull and his hospital, Dr. Rhodes and the Community Hospital, the family-owned Betts-Koenig Lumber Company (later Betts-Sine), the winter quarters of the

A.G. Barnes Circus, Stern's Famous Barbecue, and a dog-racing track at the west end. Washington Boulevard was known as the "great white way."

Culver City had its own airport in the 1920s. It was located at the intersection of what is now Slauson and Jefferson. The Culver Airport advertised flying and gliding lessons, and Harry Culver kept his plane there.

To provide monies for acquiring, erecting, and equipping an adequate city hall, a city hall fund was created. By 1924 the city offices had been relocated to Van Buren Place so that Harry Culver could build his landmark six-story Hunt Hotel, later known as the Culver Hotel. It was advertised in 1928 as having "150 Modern Rooms and Apartments, Built for You to Enjoy." The Meralta Theatre, owned by Pearl Merrill and Laura Peralta, was moved to new, larger quarters on Culver Boulevard nearby. Will Rogers acted as the master of ceremonies, and Thomas Ince provided the film *The Galloping Fish* for the opening. An election held in April 1924 provided for the issue of $75,000 of bonds for a city hall, a $50-a-month salary for the trustees, and bonds for a water system for Culver City. The following year, the city hall figures were revised to $125,000. Walter Shaw was appointed special traffic and motorcycle officer

Calpet's Studio Super Service Station, at the corner of Washington Boulevard and Jasmine, entertained much business in its time. Courtesy, Culver City Historical Society

RIGHT: A. G. Barnes Circus' winter home, located on Washington Boulevard near Sawtelle, housed many large animals such as elephants and "the largest hippopotamus in the world." Today, in their backyards, residents can still find rings once used to tie down the large animals. Courtesy, Culver City Historical Society

BELOW RIGHT: For a short time Harry H. Culver maintained offices in the former Hunt Hotel, a six-story building at the intersection of Washington and Culver boulevards. The 1924 structure is now known as the Culver Hotel. Courtesy, Seaver Center for Western History Research, Natural History Museum of Los Angeles County

for $175 a month (he later became the chief of police), and a city manager was hired that year.

The short-lived horse-racing track between Culver and the creek became the "Speedway," with its famous banked board track where Barney Olefield raced. It was billed as the fastest board track in the world. On December 15, 1924, the trustees commended the Culver City Police Department for the "efficient manner at which crowds at the auto races 12-14-24 were handled." There were more than 50,000 visitors in attendance and not a single mishap. At that event, opening day, Bonnie Hill took the top honors in the 250-mile inaugural race. He averaged 126.9 mph. Since all was going well, the trustees allowed the sale of box lunches to accommodate the crowds. That same month, they authorized payment of $50 out of the "Music and Promotion Fund" to prepare for an advertising float in the Pasadena Floral Parade (now known as the Tournament of Roses Parade), January 1, 1925.

Also in 1925 the board president was authorized to enter into a lease agreement with Camillo and Marie Louise Cereghino for a library building. Camillo Cereghino later donated the rent back to the city. The city's advertising contract with the *Culver City Call* was awarded to another newspaper, the *Cul-*

ver City Star. Eugene Donovan had begun his publishing business, the News Printing Company, three years before, but 1925 marked the beginning of his award-winning *Citizen* newspaper. By 1929 the Citizen Building was completed. (It was the first building in Culver City to be listed on the National Register of Historic Places.) Run later under the direction of Donovan's son Roy and grandson Roy, the business continues to be family owned.

In 1925 Dr. Foster Hull built the first hospital in Culver City. It was located in the Hull Building, at the corner of Watseka and Cul-

ver Boulevard. Sada's Flowers and Freeman's Grocery Store operated nearby. Store owner Louis Freeman eventually bought the Hull Building in the 1930s with Depression dollars. The American Legion completed its clubhouse on Hughes and opened the first pool in the area that year. Locals remember all of the dances sponsored there, and although it is owned by Brotman Medical Center today, the new owner refurbished it to become an historic site. The land was originally donated by Harry Culver.

In 1925 Washington School was built. Plans were approved for the Central Fire Station that same year, and the citizens voted for two propositions that resulted in the issue of bonds for $185,000. The city hall, including

police department offices, totaled $126,000, with the fire station representing the remaining $59,000. The architect selected to design the city hall was Orville Clark, and contractor R.P. Davidson's lowest bid for $95,000 was accepted. In May of that year, First Street was changed to Overland Avenue. It was also during this time that Del Rey Boulevard, also known as Putnam, became Culver Boulevard.

The year 1925 also saw the annexation of the area known as Culver West. This is the famed "finger" of the city, which extends to Walnut Avenue, one block east of Lincoln Boulevard. The property on Walnut was the site of the race track famous for dog racing. Pari-mutuel betting took place at this location, contributing to the city's reputation for

Culver City's City Hall was dedicated in 1928. Posing for this picture are city officials. The building has since been demolished to make way for the new Civic Center. Courtesy, Culver City Historical Society

gambling. It has been suggested by many that Culver City wanted this land so that all of the businesses along Washington Boulevard could be added to its economic base. Others believe that the dog track was the great interest.

A Parks, Playground and Art Commission, established in August 1927, proposed that the first park be called "Victory Park." The board of trustees had come to be known as the city council, and Mayor Reve Houck and his

council agreed to name the park accordingly. Houck's wife, Lillian, suggested it be called Victory Park because "it was a victory that there was finally a park in Culver City!" (Media Park, for which Harry Culver conducted a naming contest, became a part of Los Angeles.) Mayor Houck, who had been police commissioner in 1924, appointed a Citizens' Police Commission in 1928. City records list its first members as Mr. Hall, (Hall Motor Company), Eugene Donovan, (News Printing Company), Thomas Sauerbutts, Al Hodges, and Charles Ellis.

The fire station and city hall were completed in 1928, although the council chambers were used for the first time on February 11, 1929. Growth of the new city mandated the creation of a planning commission by resolution on November 26, 1928. That year Culver City established its own municipal bus and transportation system.

People came for miles around to skate in the new Rollerdrome to live organ music played by Mr. Osterloh. The presence of uniformed attendants cutting through with their

BELOW: The Citizen *was one of seven newspapers to operate during the 1920s, but was one of only two to survive by the end of the decade. The Citizen Building was recently named a historic site. Courtesy, Culver City Historical Society*

RIGHT: The Hull Building, the site of the first hospital in Culver City, is now one of the city's historic sites. The building today houses Riccardo's Restaurant. Courtesy, Culver City Historical Society

fancy movements helped maintain order as the bells rang and the scenarios changed. A lighted board signalled, "All Skate," "Reverse Skate," "Couples Only," "Ladies Only," or "Clear the Floor." It was a popular place for birthday parties or just to meet friends and have fun.

Culver City government in this era was proactive. The city fathers not only went about the business of providing for necessary services, like police and fire, street sweeping, paving, sidewalks, and lighting, but they also took stands to protect their community. For example, in May 1921 the trustees passed a resolution endorsing the "Save the West" campaign, which asked Congress to reconsider the Transportation Act of 1920. They felt the act stifled industry in California. The next year the city attorney was directed to "take immediate legal steps to secure relief from the nuisance [raw sewage] from intolerable conditions caused by the failure of the

City of Los Angeles to abate the nuisance in Ballona Creek." Then, by resolution in 1923, the city expressed displeasure with the state, which was two years late in utilizing the census to achieve reapportionment. The wording of the resolution was pointed at best, calling "this outrageous delay, outrageous to the basic political rights of the American citizenry . . . is resulting in an inequity between representation and taxation, in flagrant violation of the theory of all American government . . . " The local government continued its proactive stance when, in 1925, the trustees, by resolution, encouraged the UC Board of Regents to consider their Westwood campus a permanent location for UCLA, and, the following year, all city department heads were asked to resign to accomplish a "clean sweep." The council then instructed the city attorney to file a $200,000 suit against the City of Los Angeles for damage done by floodwaters from one of its storm drains.

City officials pose during the 1927 ground-breaking ceremony for City Hall. Mayor Reve Houck is seen in the center. Courtesy, Culver City Historical Society

The people of the city were also proactive. In 1929 they showed their displeasure with the council by trying to recall all of the members. Though the signatures were insufficient, this would not be the last time the recall process would be used in Culver City.

During this early development period, the movie studios grew to make Culver City the "Heart of Screenland." They lured prominent visitors like Herbert Hoover, Charles Lindbergh, and kings and queens to Culver City. Although Thomas Ince had established Triangle Studios, forming an alliance with D.W. Griffith and Mack Sennett in 1915, he only stayed long enough to build the landmark colonnade, a two-story administration building fronting on Washington, and a few glassed-in stages, with sheds serving as shops. The first movie produced was *Civilization,* and the actors who graced those glass stages included William S. Hart, Olive Thomas, Willard Mack, Leo Carrillo, Charles Ray, Billie Burke, Lew Cody, and Dorothy Dalton.

By 1918 Samuel Goldwyn had purchased the studio and added more stages and structures. Although Goldwyn sold out, his name and his trademark "Leo the Lion" with "Ars Gratia Artis" (Art for Art's Sake) remained a part of the studio name when he sold it in 1924.

Few people are privy to the Leo story. A young Howard Dietz dropped out of Columbia University as a senior and went to work for The Phillip Goodman Agency in New York. The rest of the office had failed to come up with a trademark for the Samuel Goldwyn Pictures Company. Dietz toyed with Columbia U's lion and added the Latin phrase. Dietz's idea became one of the most recognizable trademarks ever.

The new studio was called Metro-Goldwyn-Mayer, with Louis B. Mayer and the young genius Irving Thalberg in charge of production for the next 12 years. Thalberg had been credited with redirecting the West Coast division of Universal, from shooting westerns and serials to producing such memorable hits as the *Hunchback of Notre Dame.* Under the leadership of Mayer and Thalberg, MGM produced its first movie, *Ben Hur,* which turned out to be one of the greatest grossers of all time. More money went into this epic than into any picture made up to that time, and when Louis B. Mayer accompanied director Fred Niblo to shoot on location in Italy, few believed that the company would

City officials watch as the nation's flag is raised at the opening ceremonies of the Culver City Rollerdrome. Courtesy, Culver City Historical Society

even make its money back! MGM turned its small stable of box office stars, including Mae Murray, John Gilbert, Lillian Gish, Lon Chaney, Ramon Novarro, and Antonio Moreno, into an assemblage prompting the MGM slogan: "More stars than there are in the heavens."

Not only were there great actors at MGM, their early promising directors included Hobart Henly, Fred Niblo, King Vidor, John M. Stahl, Robert Z. Leonard, and Jack Conway. The studio defied the belief that war pictures would fail and produced *The Big Parade,* which set box-office records. In that first year of MGM, Mayer discovered a young Swedish actress in the movie *Gosta Berling.* This find was the first of many. Her name was Greta Garbo. Nicholas M. Schenck became president after Marcus Loew died in 1927. Moving from nickelodeons to movies, Loew had headed the studio whose initials would become the most famous in the world: MGM. The company continued to grow. In 1928 its first "part talkie," was *Alias Jimmy Valentine,* followed by Norma Shearer's starring role in the first all-talking picture, *The Trial of Mary Dugan.*

At the end of 1917, Thomas H. Ince, divested of his interest in the lot that would become MGM, had moved east to 9336

Washington Boulevard and purchased 14 acres. Ince produced movies on leased sites until his new studio was completed in 1919. The first building was the colonial "mansion" that housed his administration offices. It had dressing rooms in the rear. President Woodrow Wilson visited the new studio, as did the King and Queen of Belgium in 1920. In these early years, stars working on the lot included Florence Vidor, Charles Ray, and Dorothy Dalton. Irvin Willat, Fred Niblo, John G. Wray, and Lloyd Ingraham were just a few of the directors. Early films were *Skin Deep, The Hottentot, A Man of Action,* and *Scars of Jealousy.* Twenty-nine productions were scheduled for 1924-1925. A new, 52,000-square-foot stage was completed, and First National Producers used the studio with Ince. Ince began to release "Regal Pictures." Hunt Stromberg Productions was on the lot, and negotiations were taking place between Ince Productions and William Randolph Hearst's Cosmopolitan Company.

On November 19, 1924, Thomas Ince died unexpectedly; on the 29th, his wife, Eleanor, who was vice president of the company, took over temporarily. In January 1925 Cecil B.

deMille arranged to purchase the studio with Pathe backing. Harry Culver spoke at the dedication the following month. During his tenure in Culver City, deMille was honored by the trustees with an appointment as a "Special Police Officer." In 1928 the property became the Pathe Studios. *Geraldine* was filmed in 1929 with talking sequences. Other films made that year included *The Awful Truth* with Ina Claire, *Paris Bound* with Ann Harding, and *Big News* with Carole Lombard.

The same year Ince opened his second Culver City studio, 1919, Hal Roach Studios was established farther east on Washington. This studio remained Roach property until it was sold to become an industrial tract in 1963. A marker placed by the "Sons of the Desert" in a parkette at National and Washington recalls the Hal Roach Studios as the "Laugh Factory to the World." This studio charmed us all with Spanky and Alfalfa in The Little Rascals, Our Gang Comedies. Laurel and Hardy and the Keystone Kops, who began there, were familiar sights on city streets when shooting "on location."

In these years, moviemaking was in the air in Culver City and the surrounding area.

20th Century-Fox located just north of the city, and some of the smaller studios included Kalem, Essanay, the Willat Studio, and Foy.

An enigma to Culver City residents at this time was the "Egyptian House." It seems that a very distinctive and lavish home was constructed on Lucerne, a little east of Duquesne above La Ballona Creek. The owner, an elusive Mr. Brown who was described as a very pleasant and a very rich man, was rumored to have built the house for an Egyptian princess. It had a pool and a large swimming pond next to the creek, and its doors were equipped with gold locks. The house was shamefully ornate, even boasting a colorful mural with nudes on the bedroom ceiling. Mothers warned their children to stay away from the house. Mr. Brown's princess never arrived. Some say she died on the ship on her way to marry Mr. Brown. Nevertheless, Mr. Brown maintained his residence nearby but never actually

ABOVE: MGM's world-famous trademark, "Leo the Lion," made his roaring debut in the mid-1920s. Courtesy, Turner Entertainment Co.

RIGHT: Excitement reached a high in Culver City when aviator Charles Lindbergh visited the area. Courtesy, Alene Houck Johnson

occupied the house. It was used as apartments in its deteriorating years, and is rumored to have been a gambling hangout owned by Frank Sebastian before that. Its demise came in later years, when, in a state of decay, it was burned by the Culver City Fire Department, for practice.

Culver City's incorporation was followed by the 18th Amendment, which spelled Prohibition. The new little city earned a reputation for glitzy nightclubs, bootlegging, and gambling in the 1920s and early 1930s. According to retired Fire Chief John Kearney, Washington Boulevard in those days was the Sunset Strip of Los Angeles County. It was lined with clubs like Frank Sebastian's Cotton Club, the Green Mill, Casa Mañana, Happy Bungalow, the Nightingale Cafe, Lyon's Den, and the Kit Kat Club, as well as the Plantation Cafe and the Monkey Farm, which had flashing lights. It was such a lucrative business that Roscoe "Fatty" Arbuckle contracted with Dan Coombs to build his Plantation Cafe within a month. In 28 days the new club was completed across from La Ballona School, where Arbuckle had been a student, and its circular drive was adorned with the club's name spelled out in flowers.

This was a town known for its Vegas-style entertainment. Some famous acts included Harry James, Benny Goodman, Duke Ellington, Guy Lombardo, and Louis Armstrong (who lived on Wade Street at one time). Floor shows flaunted lines of leggy chorus girls. Gambling took place in back rooms, and drinks could easily be "fortified." The Cotton Club was in Culver City, but the kitchen was in Los Angeles, so the booze was just moved from one to the other if either city's police decided to visit. In an attempt to maintain control, the Board of Trustees passed a resolution in 1922 stating there was to be no dancing in cafes and restaurants after 11:00 p.m. In 1928 Ordinance No. 293 prohibited "the shaking of dice for money, merchandise or credit and certain games." It was a law enforcement nightmare. Police were said to be disorganized, and city officials were subject to great criticism over the handling of issues. The head of the Ku Klux Klan was even rumored to be closely tied to the police department, although the crosses burned on the hill and on the grass on Madison Avenue may have been related to a dispute over slot machine territory. The new little city was taken advantage of while it was "getting its act together."

LEFT: Frank Sebastian, flamboyant in his dress and business dealings, became well-known for his Cotton Club, which was located at Washington and National. It became Culver City's crème de la crème of nightclubs. The Cotton Club offered its big entertainers private balcony-level dressing rooms and its patrons luxurious service. Before it was destroyed by fire in 1950, the Cotton Club went through a few name changes. Courtesy, Culver City Historical Society

BELOW: In the 1920s Washington Boulevard became the "Sunset Strip" of Culver City, when the main drag housed swanky nightclubs such as Frank Sebastian's Cotton Club, the Plantation Cafe, and the Green Mill Cafe, pictured here. Courtesy, Seaver Center for Western History Research, Natural History Museum of Los Angeles County

3 *Quiet on the Set*

BY THE BEGINNING OF THE 1930S, THE MOVIE INDUSTRY IN CULVER CITY was firmly established and flourishing. In fact, in 1934 the *Citizen* ran a contest to rename the city, offering a prize of $10. Some entries were "Cinema City," "Filmville," and "Roosevelt."

Movies made in Culver City's studios often said "Made in Hollywood," a point that became a thorn in the side of Culver's citizens. The June 12, 1937, edition of the *Motion Picture Herald* carried a story of the Hollywood plan to thwart Culver City's proposal. The Hollywood and Culver City Chambers of Commerce went head to head as petitions were circulated in Culver City to change the name of the city to "Hollywood." The effort was unsuccessful. So, that year, the chamber adopted the slogan "Where Hollywood Movies are Made."

The official city seal, adopted in 1936, consisted of a shield set in a circle and divided into four quadrants, one with the California Golden Bear, the second with a sprig of lantana (the city flower adopted in 1929), the third with a rising sun, and the fourth, in the upper left quadrant, with motion picture camera equipment. Inscribed across the seal are the words: "The Heart of Screenland." That seal, proof of the importance of the movie industry, is still used today.

MGM acquired more property, which eventually gave the studio six lots on 180 acres. The *Citizen* reported in 1930 that the MGM switchboard was the largest in the West.

The death of young Irving Thalberg in 1936 saddened the industry, and the new million-dollar administration building carried his name. In the meantime, MGM was busy making films, some destined to become classics, such as *Grand Hotel, The Thin Man, Mutiny on the Bounty, The Good Earth, The Wizard of Oz, Boys Town,* and *The Philadelphia Story.* And the cameras just kept rolling.

Ince's second studio underwent changes, including the addition of the "40 acres" back lot. In an austerity move prompted by the Depression, RKO allowed the studio to be used by independent companies. A merger yielded RKO-Pathe, which then became Selznick International Studios. Here *Gone With the Wind, Little Lord Fauntleroy, King Kong, A Star is Born, Prisoner of Zenda,* and *Intermezzo* were made in the 1930s.

Hal Roach Studios, known for its comedies, was christened "Fort Roach" after the United States' entry into World War II. It seems that a General Henry ("Hap")

Gene Kelly's never-to-be-forgotten musical number from Singin' In The Rain *is another MGM classic. © 1952 Turner Entertainment Co. All Rights Reserved*

Hal Roach, Master of Entertainment

Hal Roach's circuitous route from his birthplace in Elmira, New York, to California took in Seattle and Alaska, before he traveled down to the Los Angeles area. In an interview in January 1991, shortly after his 99th birthday, Roach reminisced about the road that led him to become a producer.

He left school at the age of 16 to take a job with the railroad "weigh mail" to get to the World's Fair in Seattle. He arranged to visit his aunt there, and a girlfriend in Elmira wrote to an uncle who owned a sand and gravel company. Shortly after Roach went to work for the company, he accidentally started a fire that "took until dark to put out." That job quickly became a part of his past, and he looked on to Alaska, where workers were needed to build the railroad. He climbed aboard a boat thinking he would work a week and make enough money to return before his ticket expired. The harsh reality was that it would take his first month's pay to buy the boots he needed. He and two others sneaked off board at what was then the little-known port of Val Dez. They found out that the job was 130 miles away. Roach stayed and kept getting better jobs, but his homesickness got the best of him. He returned to Seattle the following spring, where he landed a job driving a horse-

Courtesy, Ninon DeRosa

drawn wagon for an ice cream company.

The World's Fair the year before had left people in Seattle without jobs. Hal Roach worked for $25 a month for three months when only married men were kept on the payroll. He was hired back in the spring, when the company bought a "White" truck, which was designed to do the work of four teams. He left the ice cream company to work for the White Com-

pany as a demonstrator. White sold 16 trucks to haul pipes and equipment in the Mojave Desert. Roach asked to go on the trip. In Seattle, where it rained all winter, trucks got stuck in the mud, and young Hal was known for his skill in getting them out. His boss said "Hal, if you go to LA, you won't see a drop." Not only were there no mud puddles, the trucks did not last two months in the desert!

Hal Roach's next job was with Mahoney Brothers, a contractor. He became the superintendent of freighting, in charge of mules and horses. The trucks were routed from Lancaster to Bakersfield to San Pedro. It was during this time that he noticed an ad: "Men wanted in western costume." They were asked to meet at 7:00 a.m. in front of the post office. The pay was one dollar a day plus lunch. Roach remembers having a concern that he "hadn't been on horseback in four months," but he bought himself cowboy boots, a Stetson hat, and a bandana. His job took him to Universal Studios. It was there, standing on a saloon set with a roulette table, that he noticed the crew rolling the ball and spinning it the same way. When Roach shared his limited experience at roulette, they corrected the motion and he was told, "Be here at 8:00 a.m. You're an actor now." The pay went up to $5 a day, and his workday was shortened to 8:00 a.m. to 4:00 p.m. Hal Roach remembers that when he found out what they paid in the picture business, it took him one year to go from an extra to actor to assistant director to director. In little more than 12 months, he owned his own production company. Hence, Hal Roach the producer.

Hal Roach's days as a producer began in 1914, when he launched Harold Lloyd's career as Willie Work in a number of shorts. Roach was noted as "Mack Sennett's nearest rival as a producer of comedy films" in the *Dictionary of Film Makers*. Hal Roach worked out of a studio in downtown Los Angeles, where the music center now stands. As Roach tells it, he wanted to build his own studio on a whole square block, but the area he chose became a number-one fire district where studios were not allowed. So he called Harry Culver, because there were already two studios in Culver City. The land was $1,000 an acre, so he bought 10 acres, later adding seven more. He built an apartment on the lot for his parents, and after his father died, Roach relocated his mother to a house nearby.

Hal Roach lived on Lake Street, moved to Berkeley Square, then Beverly Hills, and then to his Bel-Air home. His first wife, Margaret, threw incredible parties at the Beverly Hills home, honoring such famed personalities as Mary Pickford, John Barrymore, H.L. Hunt, Marion Davies, and Irving Thalberg. Ronald Reagan was a frequent guest. A predictable uninvited guest was Margaret Hamilton (the Wicked Witch in *The Wizard of Oz*), who used to come across the alley, take a plate of goodies, and return the dish the next morning with a thank you note! Roach's two children, Hal Roach, Jr., and Margaret, are no longer living. He married again at the end of World War II, and although this wife also died, he enjoys his three daughters by this marriage and their families.

Hal Roach Studios produced 50 comedies a year plus features. Although he principally made comedies, he also did serials for Pathe and some work for MGM. He always loved "Our Gang" and "Laurel and Hardy" comedies and calls Harold Lloyd "the best comedian, second only to Chaplin." He states that Lloyd's pictures made Hal Roach "enough money to build the studio." When asked what he enjoyed, he responded, "When I went to a preview and it was good!"

Hal Roach became a widely recognized producer of quality, family entertainment. He won his first Oscar in 1932 and an honorary Oscar in 1983, presented "in recognition of his unparalleled record of distinguished contributions to the motion picture art form." In 1990 Loyola Marymount University established an annual "Hal Roach Entertainment Award," a validation of his commitment to family entertainment. At the age of 98 he quit smoking, a habit he had since childhood. At 99 he still likes to entertain, tell stories, play bridge, and take his hunting dogs down to Chino, where he shoots birds. A founder of the Santa Anita Race Track, he still attends a few races, although he does not bet much. Frances Hilton, the widow of Baron Hilton, is his "steady date." Asked if he would do it all again, the centenarian quickly answered, "Yes, if I could have the same luck!"

When Culver City became the center for moviemaking, it drew many politicians and businessmen to the area. Here gum czar William Wrigley (left) poses with Mayor Reve Houck during the 1930s. Courtesy, Alene Houck Johnson

Arnold, commander-in-chief of the Army Air Forces, decided that films could best train recruits. Arnold reasoned that since most filmmakers were concentrated in the Los Angeles area, he would turn to the experts rather than try to reinvent the wheel. It all started with Jack Warner, but as the program grew (and as Hal Roach's Studio was idle), the action moved to Culver City. Rather than be drafted, industry professionals were urged to

work on training and propaganda films. They were permitted to enlist directly into the needed units and required to undergo an abbreviated basic training program. Young actors such as Ronald Reagan and Alan Ladd became some of the Fort Roach soldiers in the Army's First Motion Picture Unit.

The movies brought more than famous visitors to town. For the filming of *The Wizard of Oz*, 124 "Little People" were hired. This first gathering of so many Little People was reportedly the motivation behind the organization of The Little People of America. Jerry Maren, who played one of the Lollipop Kids, recalled his experiences in Culver City at "A Celebration of the Movies," a Culver City Historical Society fund-raiser in 1989. Maren remembered arriving about 1:00 a.m. on November 11, 1938. He had never seen another Little Person, except for once in a movie. To be in *The Wizard of Oz* was exciting enough, but this just added to it. Maren shared a room at the Culver Hotel, where most of the "munchkins" were housed. Others stayed across the street at the Adams Hotel. He recalled awakening in the morning to the music of a marching band. Thinking it was a welcome parade, Maren roused his two roommates, only to look out the top floor window and see uniformed servicemen . . . and their Armistice Day Parade. Jerry Maren, who loved to sing and dance, was

proud to tell his mother that he was "the one with the lollipop" in the movie. He continued to work in the industry after *The Wizard of Oz*, playing "Buster Brown" and "Little Oscar" in commercials, and occasionally working on the same show with his wife, Liz.

Although moviemaking thrived, there were no annexations to the city again until 1943. The studios continued to be the major employer until joined by Helms Bakeries and, in the 1940s, by Hughes Aircraft and later, McDonnell Douglas. Hughes, where the Spruce Goose was built, was actually located outside the city limits, but it carried a Culver City mailing address. In the "Progress Edition" of the *Evening Star News* in 1947, Senator John Cain, (R) Washington, described the "flying boat" after viewing it: "It's more fantastic inside than out. If it flies—and I hope it will fly—it will bridge the gap between the practical and reasonable and the impossible and unbelievable."

The studios also provided side jobs for the local residents. Selznick's *Ben Hur* held the record for extras at 1,500, until MGM shot *A Tale of Two Cities* with 1,800. Retired Batallion Chief Ray Moselle recalls working with all of the other off-shift Culver City firemen and

LEFT: Culver City's official seal, adopted in 1936, is still in use today. The shield is divided into four quadrants: the state bear, a sprig of lantana (the city flower), a rising sun, and a movie camera. Courtesy, Culver City Chamber of Commerce

BELOW: The Willat Studio, which gained popularity in Culver City in the early 1920s, eventually faded. It was later moved to a residential area in Beverly Hills, where it still stands. Courtesy, Culver City Historical Society

Many small studios have come and gone in Culver City, but one of the bigger motion picture studios that ranks high with MGM, United Artists, and Desilu, is RKO-Pathe. Courtesy, Culver City Historical Society

about six companies from the Los Angeles Fire Department on the "burning of Atlanta" scene for *Gone With the Wind*. Starting at 7:00 p.m., they worked for some three nights, earning $25 a night for their work on Selznick's back lot. Some very "creative" citizens were placed on the studio payroll. One fellow who lived near one of the studio lots developed a habit of starting his tractor in the evening when the studio was filming. He was paid just to be quiet.

To the east of MGM was the "back alley," where a number of businesses catered to the studio trade. People hung out in the pool hall for casting calls, and a restaurant by the name of Nancy's had Clark Gable and other stars as patrons. The "Retake Room" later became a favorite spot for movie people to con-

gregate. Across the street from the front of the studio, at Jasmine and Washington, was a garage owned by red-haired actor Charles Bickford. Sympathetic to the plight of aspiring actors, he offered them jobs when they were between parts. One could also see successful actors there such as Gary Cooper in his Dusenberg or Clark Gable in his pink Packard Roadster.

Dan Patacchia, who is known as the "Mayor Emeritus" of Culver City, came to the Los Angeles area in 1941. After a short stint with Lockheed, he became a limousine driver for the studios. Dan said working for the studios was very exciting, pointing out that most who came from the East were "a little star struck." He drove such greats as David O. Selznick, whom he called a "genius in his

LEFT: A milestone was set in 1924 when the Metro Company, an independent firm operating on Cahuenga Boulevard, the Louis B. Mayer Studios in East Los Angeles, and the Sam Goldwyn Company joined to form Metro-Goldwyn-Mayer. Pictured here is one of the lots. Courtesy, ©1987 Metro-Goldwyn-Mayer Pictures, Inc.

BELOW: MGM's Irving Thalberg Building was constructed in the 1930s and housed the administration offices for the company. The million-dollar building is dedicated to Louis B. Mayer's right-hand man, Irving Thalberg, who was only 22 years old when he was hired by Mayer to direct his studio production. Courtesy, Culver City Historical Society

field," and Alfred Hitchcock, whom he described as "a very nice, generous person." Among the stars he picked up for parties and premieres were Cary Grant, Ava Gardner, and Jennifer Jones. Fluent in Italian, Patacchia was assigned to Rossano Brazzi, who brought his own olive oil from Italy. (Dan was sure of that because Brazzi gave him a quart.) When asked who impressed him most, Dan easily answered, "Gregory Peck," saying that he "liked him as a person. He was a gentleman—off screen and on." Driving a limousine in the movie industry meant that Patacchia had to take it home with him, since he was always on call. His job often entailed picking up models at the airport for screen tests, delivering scripts, and even taking children to their doctor's appointments. Patacchia said he "made good money," generally getting paid "golden time almost every week." By 1948 he worked part-time in real estate, and two years later, built his own office on Overland Avenue. He still maintains space there.

Many local residents and visitors discovered that collecting autographs was a great way to pass the time. A prime location was MGM's East Gate, facing Madison Avenue. When Virgie Tinger (now Eskridge) wasn't helping her parents at Culver City Flowers,

she spent time getting the signatures of stars such as Jackie Cooper, Walter Pigeon, Edna Mae Oliver, and others. She was amazed when, years ago, one of her friends sold an autograph book for $450!

In 1935 the city went to bat for the movie industry by passing a resolution showing its opposition to a heavy state tax it felt would drive out the industry. The document sent to the state referred to "Culver City, home of MGM, RKO-Pathe, Hal Roach and Foy Studios, which employ large numbers of local residents, and studio payrolls provide a large percent of the city's revenue." The next month Louis B. Mayer predicted that movies would flee from California because of taxation. The bill in question was tabled a week later. That year the MGM Studio Employees Picnic drew a crowd of 5,000.

With the Depression came the demise of the 1st National Bank of Culver City, at the corner of Washington and Van Buren; bank customers received 10 cents on the dollar. Although it was a difficult time for most, a sense of community prevailed. Each teacher at Culver Grammar School donated at least $25 per month to benefit less fortunate children. The school nurse dispensed cafeteria food, clothing, and shoes to children in need. School Board Member Pearl Merrill bought rose bushes for the front of Culver Grammar School. She was also well known for spending her own time and money to visit prospective teachers, even if they lived out of state.

Industry became a prime focus for the city in the 1930s and 1940s. Helms Bakeries completed its construction in 1932 despite some serious opposition. Alene Houck Johnson recalls that many residents voiced a concern that the plant would bring an unwanted element to town. Yet the famous bakery emerged as a major employer, and the "whistle" of Helms Bakery trucks became a familiar and welcome sound. When the Olympics came to Los Angeles, Helms provided some of the breadstuffs; hence the slogan "Helms Olympic Bread." In fact, one of the Olympic villages was located up on the Baldwin Hills, just outside the city (where Kenneth Hahn Park is now). A perfect example of the confusion caused by the irregular city boundary was that Paul Helms, Jr., could sit in his office and be in either Culver City or Los Angeles, depending where his chair was located.

Another familiar sound was the music of the Good Humor trucks, letting children know the ice cream man was in the neighborhood. Not quite as pleasant, however, was the sound of the curfew siren, which sounded be-

ABOVE: Rhett Butler, played by Clark Gable, comforts a distraught Scarlett O'Hara on the death of her husband. Gone With the Wind*'s most memorable scene for studio employees was the "Burning of Atlanta," in which instead of recreating a Southern set, production executives suggested burning down the back lot. The Culver City Fire Department was on stand-by, but with director David Selznick's sprinkler system, which was installed specifically for this scene, and the cooperation of MGM's fire department, Culver City was never in danger, reported Fire Chief Bill Kuehn. © 1939 Turner Entertainment Co. All Rights Reserved*

tween 9:30 and 10:00 p.m. from the top of the fire station. Mothers complained that the signal awakened their sleeping children.

On LaFayette, just south of Culver, one of the residents kept a couple of cows and delivered milk, with cream at the top, in a horse-drawn cart. This milkman and other small operations like his were put out of business by big firms such as Adohr Farms, which delivered milk from a large facility on La Cienega, just north of the city.

Culver City's industrial beginnings are attributed to Western Stove, which celebrated its silver anniversary in the city in 1947. An article in the *Evening Star News* in August of that year told of Western Stove's evolution from two small buildings and 20 employees in 1922 to 11 acres and 750 employees. Known for a good product, it survived the Depression, manufactured products for the war effort, and became the "oldest manufacturing plant in continuous operation in Culver City other than the motion picture studios." Western's growth was called "ample proof of business the American Way."

Adolph Steller, owner of a hardware store on Main Street, was president of the Culver City Chamber of Commerce in 1945. His chamber responsibilities included actively promoting "The Hayden Tract," the first industrial park in the city. The developer of this area was Los Angeles resident Sam Hayden, who had been a glass manufacturer in the East. By 1949 it had become a 40-acre subdivision of "modern reinforced concrete

buildings," and ads for it boasted it was "one of the finest in the West." Located at the edge of this tract was Lou Cranks' chemical company, rumored to have a distillery within. Cranks later became the well-known developer of Culver Crest.

When the Meralta Theatre burned to the ground in 1943, the war made it impossible to obtain building materials. So, ironically, the "Heart of Screenland" was without a movie theater! The city came to the rescue and allowed the use of the second-floor auditorium in City Hall as a temporary solution. The Meralta reopened in 1945. That same year a plan was revealed for the opening of a "principal theater" across the street from the city hall, and a contest was advertised to name the new theater. Built in the Moderne style with a 40-foot tower, it became known as

the Culver Theatre, and more than one of its old ushers has interesting "flashlight" stories about its loges.

During the 1930s it was fun to dress for the annual "Tom Sawyer Days." Hundreds of Huck Finns, Becky Thatchers, and Tom Sawyers could be seen around town. This event might be considered the precursor to the Fiesta La Ballona, which was established in the 1950s.

Meanwhile the Rollerdrome continued to draw crowds. Roy Donovan remembers their "Swing Shift Dances" after midnight, and Carmen Shaw Simmons remembers Roy as the "Beau Brummell of Van Buren Place." The Culver City Athletic Club, with police officer "Dusty" Cadis as its prime mover, was located above the rink. At the northeast corner of Ince and Washington was the Horseshoe

ABOVE: Washington Place and Washington Boulevard are the two main arteries seen in this 1940 aerial. The Rollerdrome is visible in the center. Courtesy, Culver City Historical Society

FACING PAGE, BOTTOM: This 1949 photo of Fire Station No. 1 shows how far the city has come since the days of its volunteer fire department. The building still exists and is in the process of being relocated next to the Meralta Plaza. Courtesy, Culver City Historical Society

Club. Many prominent locals, such as Judge Emmons, enjoyed pitching horseshoes there.

Sy Saenz' boxing arena, the Culver City Stadium, was located at Venice and Overland. Saenz used the popular sport to help many local young men, allowing them to earn their keep by sweeping the place. Mae West had a special seat for Monday Night Fights. She sat next to Pearl Merrill, one of the owners of the Meralta Theatre, and Lorene Furrow, a young teacher who later became the wife of Councilman Leroy Koos. The arena was frequented by many movie people, such as Lupe Velez, who liked a ringside seat. If her favorite fighter was not in shape, Velez was often heard yelling, "You need to chop wood!" Many famous people got their start at Saenz' boxing arena, such as brothers Nish and Kirk Kerkorian. While Nish became a professional middleweight, Kirk developed from an amateur welterweight into the man who later returned to buy MGM!

Not far from the boxing arena was Ed's Chili Parlor, owned by the Hennarty family. For 25 cents one could enjoy a complete Mexican dinner with enchiladas, beans, rice, and all the trimmings.

Baseball was a popular pastime, and there were several fields in the area: one near the boxing arena, one at LaFayette and Lucerne, one at what became Veterans' Park, and another up on Charnock Drive, north of Venice Boulevard just outside the city.

La Ballona Creek had a habit of meandering. In order to contain it, an $800,000 federal grant put the U.S. Army Corps of Engineers to work in 1935. The WPA provided employment on this project for many out-of-work locals. The paving eliminated some of the lush greenery, but the kids still managed to get down to the creek to catch polliwogs and frogs. Three wooden bridges that spanned the waterway lasted until the 1980s, when they were replaced.

In 1930 bootlegging was still rampant in Culver City, though some still argue that it should be thought of in the context of the times. One recipe for "hooch" directed: "Buy the alcohol from 'Max,' and mix it with carmel coloring. Add distilled water and oak chips, so that it is 'aged in oak.'" The outlawing of liquor had its effects all over town. Gladys Chandler, a young elementary teacher who later became a principal, thought she had heard all of the excuses for being tardy, when a little girl explained that her father's "still" blew up in their basement. She was late because she had to help her mother clean up the mess!

When the 21st Amendment repealed Prohibition in 1933, the night spots began to slide. By the 1940s, Frank Sebastian's Cotton Club had become the Casa Mañana dance hall. A *Citizen* headline read, "Riot Brings Dance Hall Closings." The 1945 article referred to "imported troublemakers" rioting in the Casa Mañana dance hall, with references to "pachukos and slick chicks of zoot suit and pork pie hat fame." Operating licenses were suspended for the Casa Mañana, Plantation, and Bert Phillips Dance Hall at that time. The "Sunset Laws" were in effect from the 1920s through the early 1950s.

And then there was the gambling problem. Raids were common to deter gambling. Headlines in the January 3, 1930, *Citizen* read: "Police Break Up Huge Crap Game; Ten are Arrested." Tom Lindsay and Cecil

Truschel were among the arresting officers. In May 1935 the council adopted a resolution to halt gambling in Culver City. The *Citizen* reported that Chief of Police Cecil Truschel received special instructions from

ABOVE and LEFT: In 1932 the Helms Bakery moved into Culver City and soon began to deliver fresh baked goods. Courtesy, Culver City Historical Society

Mayor Frank H. Dobson to inform his officers to "be on the watch for all forms of gambling, and to jail anyone violating the law." Gladys's Hot Spot was owned by sisters Gladys and Babe, who were married to two local firemen. It's said that Bugsy Siegal hung out there. Because walkathons and dance marathons were considered endurance contests, they were prohibited.

St. Augustine's congregation continued to grow. In 1926, six sisters from the order of the Daughters of Mary and Joseph came from Ireland to staff St. Augustine's school. The school was actually in Los Angeles, and the church in Culver City. A new church with a seating capacity of 700 was built in 1936. During these years the church had a close relationship with MGM, located across the street. The pastor often acted as a technical advisor, and the studios provided items such as tents for the annual church barbecue. The Machados usually cooked the meat at these fund-raising celebrations. In 1949, although not all churches were located within the city boundaries, the Culver-Palms area churches included Baptist, Christian Science, Grace Lutheran, Episcopal, Methodist, Presbyterian, United Brethren, and Jehovah's Witnesses congregations.

Culver City actively increased its parks and recreation facilities. Although the first two acres of Lindberg Park were dedicated in 1927, the park was extended to Cota Street in 1938, more than doubling its size. The major-

ABOVE: Western Stove Company had its beginning in 1922 with 20 employees. It survived the Depression by making products for the war effort and became the oldest manufacturing plant in operation in Culver City. It celebrated its silver anniversary in 1947. Courtesy, Culver City Historical Society

RIGHT: Many of Culver City's churches have existed for generations, surviving disasters, economic slumps, and Prohibition. Members of the Church of Christ were active in the 1920s in trying to stop the shenanigans of bootleggers and gamblers. Courtesy, Culver City Historical Society

ity of the 10-acre Exposition Park was acquired that same year, only to be officially designated Veterans' Memorial Park in 1949. McManus Park was authorized as a $4,000 acquisition in 1939. Culver West Park, originally West End Park, had its beginnings in 1948. The mushrooming of recreational facilities was an indication that Culver City was turning back to its family orientation. In the late 1940s the county library was located at LaFayette and Braddock and boasted 50,000 volumes. As attested by the many newspaper articles at the time, the most active organizations in town were the Woman's Club; Boy Scouts; Girl Scouts; Lions Club; Elks and Moose lodges; the Exchange, Optimist, and Rotary clubs; the YMCA; and several veterans organizations.

The Western Hemisphere Marathon was established on May 21, 1948, and a monument to its runners, located in front of the Veterans' Memorial Building, marks the start and finish line. Today the marathon is run on the first Sunday of December.

War bonds were also in the forefront of city activities in the 1940s. Support for "our boys overseas" was uppermost in everyone's mind. At the end of the war, the Culver City Veterans Employment Council was established. Kathryn Barnard was in charge of the office, which was on Culver Boulevard in the basement of the city hall. Mrs. Barnard, Gladys Chandler's sister, was a well-known and much-loved lady in town. She was dedicated to helping the veterans get back on their feet. Others rallied to help, such as the local newspapers. The *Citizen* offered free "job wanted" ads to servicemen.

In 1947 Culver City became a charter city. The charter was approved by the legislature on January 20 that year, and the papers were filed with the secretary of state the next day. A.H. Segrell was serving as mayor at the time, and the other members of the City Council were J. Roy Klots, William G. Douglas, Thomas J. Carroll, and Curtis J. Davis. George W. Stevens was the C.A.O. (Chief Administrative Officer) and Michael Tellefson, the city attorney.

By 1949 Culver City had a unified school district, with plans for junior and senior high schools. Even the MGM studio school, previously staffed by the Los Angeles Unified School District, would be part of Culver City. Property taxes would then benefit all of the schools located within the city boundaries.

The population of Culver City, which stood at 503 in the 1920 census and 5,669 in 1930, had grown to 8,996 in 1940. The city had momentum, and throughout the forties its boundaries and population continued to expand.

Danceland had its heyday during the 1920s, when Culver City was notorious for its nightlife. Courtesy, Culver City Historical Society

4 *Rolling!*

Hughes Aircraft Company employed women to handle the delicate task of manufacturing tiny semiconductors. The international company produced millions of the semiconductors annually. Courtesy, Culver City Historical Society and Hughes Aircraft Company

AS THE 1950S BEGAN, THE NATION WAS PULLING ITSELF TOGETHER, and Culver City was pitching in to help. Newspaper articles covering the Red Cross drive cited the need for blood and plasma for U.S. troops injured in Korea. The Civil Air Patrol Squadron II operated out of the Culver Airport. President Truman talked about price controls to halt inflation. More than 950 Culver City residents petitioned the City Council to consider rent decontrol. Earl Warren was inaugurated as governor of California. A local Americanism Education League was formed for the purpose of fighting communistic activities. The American Legion sponsored a "Tide of Toys Campaign" for children of war-torn Europe, which was supported by the schools, Boy Scouts, and Fox theaters. The local March of Dimes campaign actively worked toward the eradication of polio. And Culver City celebrated the sentencing of Hymie Miller and his henchmen for their gambling syndicate activities.

When Farragut School first opened its doors in January 1950, it received attention from educators all over the county. This school, which replaced bungalows and accommodated 600 students, was considered one of the nation's outstanding examples of school architecture. In its first year as a unified school district, the school system was being reorganized, with the promise of an assistant superintendent in a few months. A $4-million school-construction program was under way, as work progressed on the junior and senior high school facilities and district office. In 1954 the first all-night grad party was sponsored by the PTA for Culver High's second graduating class. That same year Bessie Freiden wrote a musical play, "Changing Partners," as a fund-raiser for lights at the high school stadium. (Bessie and husband Jimmie continued to be active citizens and were often referred to as Mr. and Mrs. Culver City.) Culver City's was a growing school district, with El Marino and El Rincon elementary schools opening in 1952 and the district's eighth elementary school, Linda Vista, ready for classes in 1959. El Rincon and Linda Vista were constructed on land dedicated by developers.

The 1960s saw the construction of the ultramodern 1,400-seat Robert Frost Auditorium next to the high school. Culver City was destined to become a model, or "lighthouse," district.

In 1950 Culver City's population was about 20,000, more than double the 1940 census. During the same time period, the assessed valuation had risen from about $14 million to $35 million, with one third of the value attributed to the movie studios.

La Ballona School was the first school in the area to replace the old wooden schoolhouse. City officials wanted to create a safer building, so they hired a contractor who, ironically, was unable to demolish the building with a wrecking ball; it was eventually destroyed with dynamite. Courtesy, Culver City Historical Society

There was concern in 1950 that the Mattoon Act had taken money from the tax rolls. Although 800 properties were still vacant, more than 2,000 parcels of property had been reported entirely abandoned. At that time the number of elected officials remained the same. There were five seats on the Civil Service Commission, but the Planning Commission had nine members, as did the Park Commission.

City Attorney Mike Tellefson drew up the Inter City Sewage Disposal Contract with the City of Los Angeles, which was signed at the end of 1951 to protect Culver City's capacity rights for the future.

Marie Machado, the widow of Jose de la Luz Machado, became a colorful figure, holding public officials accountable at City Council meetings. After her death, the Machado property on Overland Avenue was developed for housing.

By the end of the 1960s, the police department had moved out of City Hall and into its own building. The practice range for the officers was moved from the hills to the basement of the new structure, and Police Chief Eugene Mueller became well known for making everyone swell with patriotism as he led the "Pledge of Allegiance" at public gatherings.

During 1950-1951 the YMCA moved into its home on Culver Boulevard. The campaign to renovate the two-story "move-on" was spearheaded by the Exchange Club. Work parties were advertised in the newspapers, and the churches worked with the "Y" to hold a Youth Week, in celebration of the local young people. The Exchange Club also sponsored a newsstand on the corner of Cardiff and Culver for blind Culver City newsboy Clark Ray, known to friends as "Corky."

The Culver City Chamber of Commerce, spearheaded by 21 directors, was recognized in a 1951 edition of the Freedom Foundation Award-winning *Citizen* as "one of the motivating factors in the city's outstanding growth." Bill Murphy Buick furnished the chamber with a car, which became a "welcome wagon" run by a hostess. The city enacted a one-half percent sales tax for revenue. In 1956 the chamber predicted almost $100 million in retail sales for the fiscal year. In its ads, Culver Center boasted growth from its first seven stores to "45 Modern, Friendly Stores to Serve You."

After the Culver City Community Coordinating Council (5 C's) cited the need for mental health care in a 1954 study, the Culver City Guidance Clinic was established with the cooperation of the Soroptimist Club. Founded in the summer of 1958 and incorporated the next year, the clinic offered low-cost outpatient services to Culver City residents. There was an initial $5,000 grant from the city, with a medical director engaged in 1961 (funded by mental health grants, fees and donations, and a one-time,

$7,000 gift of funds from the city). The Guidance Clinic Guild was established to help support the clinic, which still exists as the Family and Child Guidance Clinic within the Didi Hirsch Community Mental Health Center. The first president of the clinic was Police Captain Charles R. Lugo, with Mary Taw serving as the first Guild president. The Guild still sponsors the annual Royal Medallion

ABOVE: During the 1950s Culver City's school system went through a reorganization phase. Construction of school facilities for the junior and senior high schools were under way, the city celebrated its first Grad Night in 1954, and by 1959 there were eight elementary schools in operation. Courtesy, Culver City Historical Society

LEFT: Ronald "Brick" Coombs, pictured at right in the foreground, was a foreman at Hall Motors on Washington Boulevard before becoming an attorney and a leading citizen. Courtesy, Ronald H. Coombs

ABOVE: Evening Star-News *employees posed for this 1956 photo outside the main entrance to the offices of the paper. Courtesy, Culver City Historical Society*

FACING PAGE, TOP: Betts *Lumber Company employees posed for this group picture. The company was located on Washington Boulevard. Courtesy, Culver City Historical Society*

Debutante Ball as its primary fund-raiser for the clinic.

In 1956 President Dwight D. Eisenhower, who visited Culver City during his presidency, initiated a program to promote peace, friendship, and understanding through people-to-people contact between countries. Culver City's "Sister City Committee" formed its first sister-city relationship in February 1964. A delegation visited the Franciscan-founded city of Uruapan in Michoacan, Mexico. Culver City's old fire engine was later driven down to Uruapan for use by its firefighters. The following year a second sister city, Kaizuka, Japan, was added. By 1990 Culver City had also established relationships with Iri City, Korea, and Lethbridge, Canada.

A sense of community brought together a group of locals to establish their own La Ballona Savings. This diverse group, which included Warren Betts (lumber), Phil Watson (later county assessor), Dave Duncan (newspaper publisher), John McCarty (plumbing con-

tractor), Bill Alberts (optometrist), and Roy M. Good (legal counsel), opened their hometown financial institution in a 20- by 80-foot building on Culver Boulevard near Main Street. By 1962, after a merger but still maintaining local autonomy, the savings and loan opened a facility on an acre of land on Washington Boulevard and Delmas Terrace. It subsequently became Financial Federation, later acquired by Great Western. George Newhouse, who operated the facility for 27 years until his retirement in 1982, maintains that the real estate market was not great early on, but that millions were made on 1st trust deeds.

In 1958 the San Diego Freeway was dedicated by Governor Edmund G. "Pat" Brown on the bridge over Washington Boulevard. Access to the San Diego Freeway and the Santa Monica Freeway, along with storm drains and an unbelievably steady climate, caused Culver City to flourish. And with the advent of the Hayden Tract and Culver Center, industry began to diversify.

The sale of the last remnant of a ranch, the Lugo property, in the 1950s gave way to the Studio Village Shopping Center. Real estate values, after all of these improvements, saw a steady appreciation. George Newhouse, whose retirement was only temporary, as he now serves as chairman of the board and CEO of Culver National Bank, remembers that there was a heavy demand for home loans.

There was a flood of financial institutions in the 1960s, and the local response was to "start their own." This time it was Charter Bank, in 1963.

Culver City also witnessed the beginning of apartment house complexes during this decade. The first condominiums were built across from the landmark Studio Drive-In on Sepulveda Boulevard in 1965; the density was

15 units per acre. The development of Palms into multifamily housing had a great impact on the area. There was a mass conversion of 50- by 150-foot lots from single homes to eight- and nine-unit apartment buildings.

BELOW: Street construction and maintenance are vital to an ever-growing city. Courtesy, Culver City Historical Society

The Venice Pier was the brainchild of visionary Abbot Kinney, a real estate entrepreneur who was first sent to California as a federal commissioner to investigate the condition of the mission Indians. After he and his partner developed the area that became Ocean Park, he wanted to beautify the city in the most grandiose manner and thus planned the construction of the 1,700-foot-long and 30-foot-wide pier. Courtesy, Culver City Historical Society

With its proximity to freeways, downtown, LAX, and employment opportunities, Palms became a popular area to live. Hence, Overland and other avenues became bottlenecks for traffic.

As the city grew, so did its need for recreational facilities. A bond issue of $550,000 guaranteed the construction of the Veterans' Memorial Building in 1950. Original plans promised a "recreational building with a stage, restaurant, film museum, playroom, and large gymnasium." The cornerstone was laid April 15, 1950, fortified with a complete history of Culver City and highlights of various civic organizations and activities throughout the year. The City Council and Park Commission participated in the ceremonies marking the start of construction on the auditorium, which was

then advertised to seat 2,000, with a tourist tower that would offer a view of "the interior of practically every movie set in the city." The lobby was reserved for valuable movie-studio curios, and the council had adopted an ordinance the previous year that would, through slant oil drilling, help defray the costs of the structure. To the delight of the citizens, the swimming pool opened within a few months. The County Library was built between the pool and the Vet's Building in the 1960s. In a cooperative effort between the city and state, the Armory was constructed concurrently with the Vet's Building, just west of Vet's Park. Culver West Park was completed in 1953, and the land for El Marino Park was purchased from Camillo and Marie Cereghino in 1954.

The Fiesta La Ballona had its beginning in

1951. A week-long celebration of the heritage of the area, it was sponsored by the city's recreation department. Activities included a parade with marching bands, floats, vintage cars, and horse-drawn carriages, a barbecue, teenage hop, square dance, modern dance, aquacade, kiddie parade, thieves market, melodrama, Fiesta Queen contest, coronation breakfast, and a hobby, art, and photo show. Residents were expected to dress for the events. Señors and señoritas were festively attired even at work, as the "pokey" picked up anyone who was not in costume. From its famed wardrobe department, MGM was known to outfit local officials. The Fiesta ran for 13 consecutive years, later to be resurrected as a weekend "Festival of the People," returning in the 1980s to a one- or two-day fiesta.

At the west end of town, local machine-shop owner George Newman remembers his "debut" in a midget auto at the track on Walnut and Washington. Television recorded "Old Leatherbritches," Dick Lane, advertising jalopies from the track that went from a 1/4-mile, banked, asphalt course to a 1/2-mile, figure-eight track. As with all Culver City landmarks, it was used in movies. The track's last phase was as a demolition derby. The property later served as the site of a McDonnell Douglas plant, a Hughes Helicopter facil-

ity, headquarters of the 1984 Olympics, a swap-meet site, and as the location of a controversial Prudential development.

There were 16 annexations to the city during the 1950s and 1960s. These included the areas that came to be known as Culver Crest, Baldwin Hills, Blair Hills, McManus Park, and Fox Hills. In the Culver Crest annexation, the city gained a hilly area that became an exclusive residential development subdivided by Lou Cranks. At the top of that hill was a mansion surrounded by avocado groves, which had been built by Los Angeles lawyer Leo

BELOW: Citizens promoting social, cultural, and civic pride sparked what is now a 40-year tradition, Fiesta La Ballona. Members of the 500 Club pose here. The fiestas were a week-long celebration that paid homage to the area's Spanish-Mexican residents. Courtesy, Culver City Historical Society

LEFT: DeWitt J. Brady was known throughout Culver City for his bus company and garage next door to Hal Roach Studios. Attorney, builder, auto racing enthusiast, Brady also owned this car dealership on Washington Boulevard. Courtesy, Culver City Historical Society

This Douglas Aircraft parking facility was originally the site of the dog-racing stadium. Located at the intersection of Walnut and Washington Boulevard, it is now the site of Culver City's Marina Place. It also housed the headquarters for the Los Angeles Olympics in 1984. Courtesy, Culver City Historical Society

Youngworth. Youngworth lost his property during the Depression, which led not only to changes of ownership but a colorful history as well. Hunting wild turkeys in the avocado groves gave way to a foreign ambassador using the mansion as a facade for gambling and bootlegging operations. It also housed royalty and such luminaries as opera singer Grace Moore. In 1945 it became the property of developer Lou Cranks, whose wife, Esther, was the sister of Tony Carnero, the owner of the gambling ship *Rex*. In 1954, after Esther died, the land was purchased by the Archdiocese of Los Angeles to become Marycrest Manor, a retirement home for elderly ladies. Marycrest Manor continues as a retirement and convalescent home today, and building additions have been made to accommodate the increasing number of senior citizens needing this type of care.

The 1964 annexation of the Fox Hills area brought two 18-hole golf courses (the Fox Hills Country Club and Baldwin Country Club) and the Red Riding Stables to the city. Flooding at Slauson and Sepulveda often caused cars to get stuck during heavy rains, leaving development options limited at that time.

With the increase in local population, St. Augustine's made plans to build a new church. Under the direction of Monsignor James McLaughlin, construction of the new

American Gothic-style church, with a seating capacity of 1,070, began in 1957. It opened its doors on Christmas that year, although the official dedication was held the following June, with Archbishop James Francis Cardinal McIntyre officiating. The schoolchildren sang for this festive occasion, which drew many dignitaries, among them the monsignor's old school chum, famous preacher and media personality Bishop Fulton J. Sheen.

It was during this period that Culver City's first synagogue was built. In 1953 Temple Akiba was located on Venice Boulevard. Planning for construction began the following year, and after occupying an interim facility on Overland and Jefferson, the congregation broke ground in 1963 for the current synagogue, which is located on Sepulveda Boulevard.

The year 1950 found the movie industry at a low ebb, with attendance at movies falling off severely. MGM had been busy filming *Annie Get Your Gun*, which became its biggest musical and moneymaker at the time. Not far from there, on lot 2, Elizabeth Taylor and Spencer Tracy were filming *Father of the Bride*. Among the other MGM films in production were *Harvey, Royal Wedding*, and *Summer Stock*, Judy Garland's swan song at MGM.

MGM's motto remained "Make it good . . . make it big . . . give it class!" Louis B. Mayer's last year as studio chief was to be 1951. The

Afternoon light adds a tranquil touch to the interior of St. Augustine's Church. St. Augustine's was named Historic Site #3 by the Culver City Historical Society. Photo by Amy Seidman-Tighe

studio doubled its TV production, and movie releases included *An American in Paris, A Streetcar Named Desire,* and *Quo Vadis,* in which Robert Taylor, Deborah Kerr, 20 "Christian-eating lions," and two cheetahs generated the best cash flow for the studio since *Gone With the Wind.* It was that same year that Humphrey Bogart won an Academy Award for his role opposite Katharine Hepburn in *The African Queen.* And Kathryn Grayson, Howard Keel, and Joe E. Brown starred in the remake of Edna Ferber's novel *Showboat,* on the lake at Lot 3.

In 1952 Cinerama opened to great public enthusiasm with a screen six times the normal size. The following year 3-D became the gimmick to see Ann Miller's legs in *Kiss Me Kate,* and the industry tried to attract moviegoers with CinemaScope, Vistorama, VistaVision, Vectograph, Vitascope, Todd-AO, Bolix-3-D, MGM's Perspecta-Sound, and others. In 1957 MGM introduced its new wide-film process (Camera 6.5) in *Raintree County*

with Elizabeth Taylor and Montgomery Clift.

In response to governmental antitrust actions, MGM-Loews divided itself into Loews Theaters and Metro-Goldwyn-Mayer in 1959. Within six months it became apparent that the split only helped the studio, as profits soared to the highest level since 1951. The year 1959 was also when Charlton Heston starred in the MGM remake of *Ben Hur,* which garnered 12 Oscars. That year also brought Alfred Hitchcock to MGM in Culver City for the first time, as he filmed Cary Grant and Eva Marie Saint in *North by Northwest.*

As the new decade emerged, it was not surprising that MGM boasted the highest gross of all studios, even though the studio only released 19 features, 12 of which were made in Culver City.

In the early 1960s the MGM lot encouraged TV production as well as film production. Some of the shows shot there included "Dr. Kildare," "Combat," "Twilight Zone," and "The Man from U.N.C.L.E."

In 1950, the year after Selznick's bankruptcy forced a liquidation of assets, Howard Hughes took over the ownership of the RKO studios on Gower in Hollywood and the RKO-Pathe site in Culver City. From 1951 to 1953 the Culver City lot was bustling with television and feature-film production. The studio was purchased by Thomas Francis O'Neill in 1955, the year David O. Selznick returned to his old lot. The studio was being used by independent television companies, and in 1956 the last RKO film shot on the lot

was made. The following year the property became the Desilu Studio.

During the 1960s independent producers kept the lot alive. Then Paramount acquired the Desilu holdings and 20th Century-Fox became a tenant. 20th's TV division shot "Peyton Place," "Felony Squad," "Green Hornet," and "Batman."

The end of the 1960s supplied a cause for celebration, as the city of Culver City celebrated its 50th anniversary in 1967. Harry Culver's widow, Lillian, came to town to celebrate. During the festivities she presented Mayor Dan Patacchia with a silver loving cup inscribed for the occasion, as the city looked forward to its 75th anniversary.

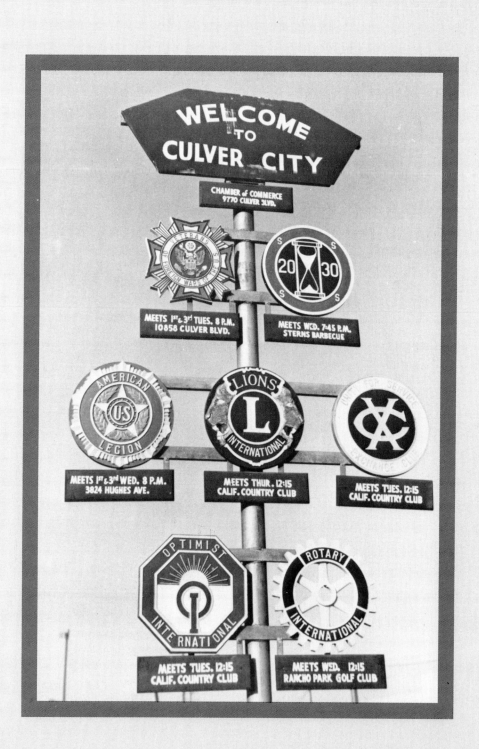

5 *Changing the Script*

BY 1970 THE ONLY VACANT LAND IN CULVER CITY LAY IN FOX HILLS, and the leading issue became redevelopment. Property values soared. The prime location, known for its climate, schools, and municipal services, continued to draw people to the city. The 1980 census tabulated the number of residents at 38,189, a 23.1 percent increase over the 1970 number of 31,035. It also showed a 42.3 percent increase in housing units during the same 10-year period.

By the end of the 1980s, the city established a Public Finance Advisory Committee (PFAC), an Historic Preservation Advisory Committee (HPAC), and Direction 21, which brainstormed Culver City into the twenty-first century. The 1950s Traffic Commission evolved into a Traffic Committee, and the Architectural Review Board, established in 1971, had disintegrated by 1975. Thousands attended a heated council meeting to watch Milton Berle attempt to bring card parlors into Culver City (he failed), and growth and building height became serious concerns. Fireworks, which had been legal since 1931, became a political issue, and in a special election in 1986, the electorate decided to eliminate them except for the special Exchange Club-sponsored 4th of July show at the high school. A Visitor's and Convention Bureau came and went, and Culver City's 1986 "Kings of Comedy" entry in the Rose Parade won the Theme Award.

Culver City has many community clubs to keep residents active. Some of the organizations are listed here. Courtesy, Culver City Historical Society

The 1970s marked the beginning of redevelopment in Culver City. The Redevelopment Agency was formed in 1971. The members of the City Council, acting as a completely different governmental entity, began to meet on alternate Mondays as the Redevelopment Agency, and established three project areas that comprise approximately one-third of the city. Because the members of the council and the agency are the same, there is continuity, a familiarity with city decisions, and fewer layers of bureaucracy.

Project One includes the Fox Hills area and some property in the Slauson/Sepulveda portion of the city. Although two hotels were first built in the area, the first major project was the redevelopment of Fox Hills. Plans were drafted, and by the end of 1975, the Ernest Hahn Company developed the Fox Hills Mall, with three anchor department stores and more than 100 shops. The sales tax collected at the mall still brings in 15-20 percent of the total annual sales tax revenue in the city. The lush landscaping behind the mall buffers it from other developments in the area. Home Savings and Loan built condominiums and apartments on the golf courses they had purchased

Pictured here is the construction of the new headquarters of the Culver City Police Department on Duquesne. Courtesy, Culver City Historical Society

privately and then closed. Upland Industries, which was taken over by Koll Center Industries, built a business park. The Redevelopment Agency was empowered to purchase 10 acres in that area for Fox Hills Park, which owed its development to the city through Quimby Act funds, designated for recreational facilities.

The Corporate Pointe section of Fox Hills was purchased and transferred in a back-to-back escrow from the state to the Redevelopment Agency to the developer, with a price tag of about $2.95 million for the raw land. Bramalea took charge, but development has been fraught with controversy over building height. Although the buildings were tapered away from the bordering Los Angeles residences to spare sun in their yards, a height initiative was filed with the city in 1988 by proponents Beverly Szabo, Robin Turner,

and Morris Marmon. The measure limited building height to 56 feet or four stories, but a lack of signatures put off voting until the 1990 April election. The measure passed by little more than a simple majority. The area is now the home of Bramalea, a Pepperdine University campus, law offices, GMT Studios, and Apple to name a few. A "restaurant row" was a desired outcome of redevelopment of the "kite" property on Hannum, across from the mall and Corporate Pointe. Failure to attract fine restaurants, however, has left the future of the property in limbo.

Redevelopment Project Area 2, which was established in December 1971, is primarily located east of Sepulveda along Jefferson/ Overland. It includes four of the old MGM lots. Lot 3, the largest, which had the famous lake, waterfront village, Western town, and St. Louis Street, was purchased by Levit and Sons

When Fox Hills Mall opened in October 1975, record sales for the rest of the year marked a profitable future for the shopping center and for the city. The mall is seen here during the final stages of construction. Courtesy, Culver City Historical Society

to became three housing developments. They are currently known as Lakeside, Tara Hills, and Raintree, which has a new lake. Lot 4 became a business park, while Lot 5 was developed into Raintree Plaza, a neighborhood shopping center. The last lot was converted into Rotary Plaza, senior affordable housing, and the offices for contractor Goldrich Kest, who built the first condominiums in the city and is responsible for senior housing next to the interim city hall. Other projects in the area will be the development of the Studio Drive-In property, additional senior housing, and boulevard realignment.

Project Area 3 was designated in 1975 and is considered to be the "downtown" area. An advisory committee, called the PAC (Project Area Committee), was mandated by state law. This committee is composed of volunteers: residents and businesspeople in the project area, representatives from community organizations, and residents of other areas. Although no longer a mandated body, the committee continues to exist as the RP3C (Redevelopment Project 3 Committee). The renovation of Culver Center from 1979 to 1983 was the first major project in this area. The Meralta Plaza is a beautiful Spanish-style commercial structure erected by Byco on the site of the Meralta Theatre; it was occupied in 1984. Because of the lack of space in the city hall, the Redevelopment Agency became tenants until the new civic center could be completed. The eight-story, $90-million Filmland Corporate Center was opened in 1985 with MGM/UA as its major tenant. This award-winning high-tech building, with 10,000 square feet of glass covering the entry atrium, immediately became a local landmark. The remaining studios are also in this project area. MGM's Lot 2 became Studio Estates and senior housing built by Goldrich Kest. The remaining land, on the corner of Overland and Jefferson, was purchased by the Redevelopment Agency as the site for the interim city hall, while the new civic center is built on the site of the old city hall.

One redevelopment project planned by private enterprise in Area 3 is The Culver Studios, which began in 1987. The main lot is completed, and a site plan has been approved for property in the next block. The

Pictured here is the off-ramp of the Marina Freeway as it passes by the Fox Hills Mall (on the far right) and exits on Slauson Boulevard. Also seen in the background are Ladera Heights and Baldwin Hills. This was also the site of the start of the marathon race during the Los Angeles Olympics. Courtesy, Culver City Historical Society

Culver Studios became a part of the Sony family in 1991. Carl Buck built the first new industrial area in the vicinity that was not agency-related. Other small projects redeveloped the Ince/Robertson area and Mike Miller Toyota-Chevrolet. The agency has a number of irons in the fire, such as the Watseka Parking Structure, which is scheduled for completion in 1992 and will be the first public parking structure in Culver City. At the eastern gateway of the city, the Ivy Substation and Media Park became part of Culver City for 40 years with an option for 10 additional years. This long-term lease was entered into with the City of Los Angeles in 1987. Culver City residents anxiously await the renovation since the structure is listed on the National Register of Historic Places, and Harry Culver's first park, which is part of the package, has become an eyesore.

Prudential purchased property in 1980 at the west end of the city, most remembered for its dog-racing track, midget autos, and aircraft plant. After five different plans were submitted to the city, the Planning Commission and City Council voted to approve "Marina Place," a shopping center with two anchor department stores, specialty shops, and six movie theaters. Despite traffic mitiga-

tion plans and community outreach, the Venice Town Council was joined by the Los Angeles City Council in a lawsuit against the project. The Coastal Commission, even though the property was outside its boundaries, filed an amicus brief, or legal statement of support. Another suit was brought by a group that splintered from the Venice Town Council. Though the judge ruled in favor of the approved private sector project in 1990, Councilmember Ruth Galanter urged the City of Los Angeles to appeal the suit, which it did. As her 1991 New Year's resolution, Galanter promised, "I will do everything in my power to stop Culver City's monstrous Marina Place shopping mall."

While redevelopment was beginning, the long-awaited senior citizens' center became a reality in 1972. The county vacated its Overland Avenue library facility to move into new, larger facilities down the street. The question was then posed, "What is the best use of the old library building?" Debates cited the proximity to the pool and Human Services Department and pointed to a variety of uses, including as a new teen center or senior center. Mary Evans, president of the Merrymakers, pleaded with the City Council, telling of the plight of local seniors, pointing to the

(text continues on page 81)

ABOVE: The landmark Filmstrip U.S.A. sculpture is illuminated in the reflection pool in front of the Veterans Memorial Building at the corner of Culver Boulevard and Overland Avenue. Photo by Amy Seidman-Tighe

LEFT: Studio Drive-In, on Sepulveda near Culver Boulevard, shines its neon lights for moviegoers of the area. Photo by Amy Seidman-Tighe

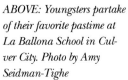
ABOVE: Youngsters partake of their favorite pastime at La Ballona School in Culver City. Photo by Amy Seidman-Tighe

ABOVE RIGHT: Children take playground equipment for a spin in Culver City Park. Photo by Larry Molmud

RIGHT: There's nothing wrong with hanging around in Culver City Park—as long as you don't let go! Photo by Larry Molmud

ABOVE: Cheerleaders gather before the front doors of the Culver City Youth Center. Photo by Amy Seidman-Tighe

LEFT: Diamonds are a boy's best friend—at least they are during a ball game at Culver City Park. Photo by Larry Molmud

FACING PAGE, TOP: Brotman Medical Center, one of the most respected and diversified medical facilities in the nation stands solidly in Culver City. Photo by Larry Molmud

FACING PAGE, BOTTOM: Palm trees and sunny, Southern California skies lend a surreal charm to this bucolic storefront in Culver City. Photo by Larry Molmud

LEFT: The sloping angles of the new headquarters of MGM cascade dramatically onto the street. Photo by Larry Molmud

BELOW: Even business complexes such as the Spanish-style Meralta Office Plaza, erected on the site of the old Meralta Theatre, keep the historic flavor of the city alive. Photo by Larry Molmud

ABOVE: Culver City is graced with a diversity of homes, from California Bungalow and Mediterranean to Colonial and the Ranch-style pictured here. Photo by Amy Seidman-Tighe

RIGHT: Three-year-old Ashley Weber takes time out from her busy day to feed the ducks at the Raintree Development Lake. Levit & Sons was the development company who masterminded the idea to build Raintree, a residential complex made up of condominiums, townhouses, and apartments. Photo by Amy Seidman-Tighe

ABOVE: When the Raintree Complex was being constructed, the developers took the existing lake and redredged it so that townhouses could be built alongside. This is the same lake that the Bounty floated upon, as well as the famous showboat from the picture of the same name. Photo by Amy Seidman-Tighe

ABOVE LEFT: Fourth of July fireworks are displayed annually by the Exchange Club at Culver High Helms Field. Photo by Amy Seidman-Tighe

ABOVE: A variety of sartorial accessories can be seen on display at Fiesta Days. Photo by Amy Seidman-Tighe

RIGHT: These seniors twirl their way through the square dance at Fiesta Days in Culver City. Photo by Amy Seidman-Tighe

impressive numbers in their clubs, the Merry-makers and Always Young. According to Jody Hall-Esser, the seniors were like "an airplane looking for a landing strip." The 23-year-old Hall was teaching at Cal State Los Angeles at the time. A USC graduate, she had also worked for the university's recreation department and had completed some graduate work in gerontology. She had learned from her father, Dr. Tillman Hall, vice-chairman of the California Commission on Aging, that there was funding available. After Culver City received a $50,000 grant in the fall of 1971, Jody Hall-Esser applied for the position of director of the senior center, and was hired in December of that year. Modifications were already under way for the restrooms, and since the library had been vacated, only a few bookshelves remained. Syd Kronenthal, the department head, gave her the needed support and the freedom to run the center as she saw fit. There were only two stipulations: The center was to be open 365 days a year, and Hall-Esser was THE STAFF, with $50,000 for salaries, equipment, supplies . . . don't overspend!

Hall-Esser worked with a planning committee and the presidents of the two senior clubs. After six months she had one part-time staff person and lots of volunteers. The community was particularly supportive, and people pitched in to solve problems and equip the center. The seniors were thrilled with their new center, which hummed with activ-

This area, where Main Street intersects Venice Boulevard, was particularly prosperous. Courtesy, Culver City Historical Society

ity. Culver City offered a model center. According to Hall-Esser, this was because they "did so much with so little, and looked to the lifelong experience of the seniors." There were few restrictions, so the center imaginatively catered to the needs of the senior population. Classes and informal lectures were offered in a variety of subjects. Puzzles, pool, and bingo offer pleasant diversion, and modestly priced trips continue to give the seniors needed getaway time. About a year after the center opened, grant funding was acquired for a Retired Senior Volunteer Program (RSVP). One of their first jobs was to take caps off pill bottles for the VA Hospital. Their "seemingly insignificant" work facilitated getting medicine to the veterans earlier, a needed help. Some seniors have racked up thousands of hours of volunteer time, working all over the city, in the library, in private businesses, and for the city.

The community is pleased to have an active senior center. The Jaycees provided a Thanksgiving dinner that has since been taken over by the Lions Club. Candidates for

local elective office enjoy participating in candidates' forums sponsored by the seniors, and there is a general respect given to the "grey panther" population, which often acts as advisors to city and school district groups. The Culver City Senior Citizen and Community Center, opened in January 1972, remains a model center.

When Jody Hall-Esser left the center in 1974 to work in the private sector, her only regret was that she hadn't been able to tackle the issue of housing for seniors. That was in the offing, however, since two years later Hall-Esser became the housing director for the City of Culver City. With the help of "Red" Betts and the Rotary Club and the Redevelopment Agency, "Rotary Plaza" was completed in the mid-1980s as low-cost housing for seniors and the disabled. That was just the beginning, and Hall-Esser, who now serves as the director of community development, is still looking to augment available housing for the senior population.

Nearly a decade after the library was transformed into a senior center, the Veterans

The Meralta Plaza, a beautiful Spanish-style commercial structure, was erected by the Byco development company on the site of the Meralta Theatre. Photo by Julie Lugo Cerra

Memorial Building was completely renovated. The auditorium floor was refinished, and wall treatments were designed for easy maintenance. The north wall of the Garden Room was rounded to facilitate the painting of a landscape mural depicting some of the old MGM facades that stood on Lots 2 and 3. After six months of work, artist Natalie Krol unveiled her seven-ton stainless-steel sculpture, *Filmstrip U.S.A.,* which sits in a 52- by 36-foot reflection pool/fountain in front of the glassed-in Rotunda Room. The $130,000 work of art was partially financed by individual and organizational contributions. "Signature tiles" were sold for the fountain's exterior. Councilman Richard Brundo spearheaded the fundraising campaign. As a special gift to the City, Krol cast a city seal in stainless steel for the Council chambers. The old painted wooden seal was hung over the newly draped stage in the auditorium.

During this period the Rollerdrome property became a neighborhood park. It was named Tellefson Park in a 1976 Bicentennial dedication. Mike Tellefson was remembered as a prime mover in the construction of recreational facilities such as the Veterans Memorial Building. His 31-year, sometimes rocky, tenure with the city included positions as CAO and city attorney. His legal expertise is still recognized with respect to the sewage contract he effected with Los Angeles for use of its Hyperion Treatment Plant.

Culver Park, located at the end of Duquesne in the Baldwin Hills, was dedicated as a 41-acre park in the 1980s. Its development was confused by controversy over the Little League fields, which were located on old oil fields in the upper section, with some pumping still in progress. City officials agreed to make the lower portion a park with equipment in keeping with an oil-drilling theme. This lower section was also chosen by the Redevelopment Agency as a site on which to relocate the Willat Studio (which was scheduled to return to Culver City as a museum). Unfortunately, the owners of the house backed out at the last minute.

To date, with the acquisition of other recreation property, such as the paddle tennis courts on Culver Boulevard, recreational acreage in Culver City totals nearly 90 acres plus a bike path to the beach along La Ballona Creek.

In the meantime, the Sister City Committee continued its pursuit of cultural exchanges. The Lions and Rotary clubs, as well as children in the school district's Spanish Immer-

Advertisements for the Biblical masterpiece Ben Hur *overlook MGM's parking lot. An MGM crew journeyed to Rome for production, but cameramen discovered the Coliseum's walls admitted too little light to photograph many of the scenes. MGM executive Irving Thalberg suggested leasing a vacant parcel of land at La Cienega and Venice boulevards to re-create Rome's past. Courtesy, Culver City Historical Society*

sion Program, make and receive visitations. After a particularly active relationship with Kaizuka, Japan, its citizens planned an incredible gift that would be visible at the front of the new library site. The area was measured for a Japanese Meditation Garden—a garden assembled in Japan, taken apart, and flown over to Culver City. The Japanese landscapers reassembled the garden, with waterwheel, lanterns, and seven tons of rock, with help from the local Japanese Center. It was dedicated in 1974.

Meanwhile, Culver City Committee members raised funds to have a stainless-steel sculpture crafted by Natalie Krol. The sculpture, *Man, Woman and Child,* was shipped to Japan, and a delegation from Culver City participated in the dedication ceremony in front of Kaizuka's city hall.

Iri City, Korea, became Culver City's third sister city in 1983. Iri is an industrial city with four times the population of Culver City. The fourth sister city relationship was formed with Lethbridge, Canada, in 1990.

A renewed relationship with Uruapan came after CAO Dale Jones and his wife vis-

ited the Mexican sister city in the late 1980s. The Sister City Committee took action to "adopt" an orphanage, the Casa de Cuna. Jones discovered that the nuns were not supported by their order or the church, and that the children had milk only once a month. A special account was established, with the interest forwarded monthly to buy milk and food. Each of Culver City's sister city affiliations has been honored by dedicating a room in its name in the Veterans Memorial Building.

Shortly before redevelopment began in earnest and Culver City turned to social and cultural matters, James T. Aubrey was placed in the top position at MGM by new owner Kirk Kerkorian. It was 1969 and MGM needed to raise money. More than 150,000 studio props, wardrobe items, and pieces of furniture were sold to the David Weisz Company for about $2 million. The famed 10-day auction began on May 17, 1970, on Stage 27, with Greta Garbo's hat bringing in $300. The Wicked Witch's Hat from *The Wizard of Oz* brought in $450, while the Cowardly Lion's suit was sold to the highest bidder at $2,400. Judy Garland's Ruby Slippers from the film appeared on the auction block. Culver City's Mayor Martin Lotz spoke, telling all present that the slippers should stay in Culver City, and the local schoolchildren had authorized him to bid the $1,000 they had raised for that purpose. Unfortunately, the plea fell on deaf ears, and the slippers were sold for $15,000. There were another six pairs, with Western Costume later producing replicas in 1990 for $5,000.

In 1970 MGM was operating at a loss and closed its studio in Great Britain. Lot 3 was used for the last time by Frank Sinatra in a rowdy Western. The 180-acre studio was reduced to two lots. The four on Overland and Jefferson were sold. MGM's financial statement in 1973 showed a net income of $9 million, but that included the sale of studio properties, overseas theaters, and music companies. In 1974 the studio's new president, Frank E. Rosenfelt, stated that "one of our principal objectives will be to provide a climate at MGM which will attract creative filmmakers . . . contrary to recent public speculation, the roar of Leo the Lion will not be reduced to a weak meow."

That May, MGM premiered *That's Enter-tainment,* a tribute to its first 50 years. It dazzled audiences with 132 minutes of prime footage from the studio archives. The following year, *That's Entertainment Part II* was well received and MGM collaborated with Columbia to effect a shared income for *The Wind and the Lion.* Industry veterans suggested the concept would not have been popular with Louis B. Mayer, but no one had even an inkling that Columbia would own the lot in the future.

From 1973 to the early 1980s, MGM was

BELOW: Carlson Memorial Park is named after Dr. Paul Carlson, a Culver City resident who lost his life in the line of duty as a medical missionary. The park was originally called Victory Park, but was later renamed in his honor. Courtesy, Julie Lugo Cerra

LEFT: These ladies enjoy stamp cutting at the Senior Citizen Center. From left to right are: Maria Contreras, Norerle Waterworth, Rose Calvert (94 years old), and Mary Evans (92 years old). Photo by Amy Seidman-Tighe

The postwar boom sparked the construction of the Veterans Memorial Building, located at the corner of Culver Boulevard and Overland Avenue. Pictured in front of the building is Natalie Krol's seven-ton stainless-steel sculpture Filmstrip U.S.A., *which sits in a reflection pool in front of the Rotunda Room. Courtesy, Culver City Historical Society*

out of the distribution business, using United Artists and UIP for that purpose. In 1981 Kerkorian bought UA from Transamerica. There was an influx of their New York people to Culver City. By the mid-1980s Kirk Kerkorian, who had trained as an amateur boxer just across from the MGM lot as a youngster (fighting at the same arena as Ted Cooke, a Venice kid who became Culver City's police chief), was to sell his movie kingdom to Ted Turner. Turner, a Georgia gentleman in the family broadcasting business who owns the Atlanta Braves and CNN, has admitted he likes to live on the edge. Turner's acquisition included the 44-acre studio lot and the film library. Turner immediately sold back UA to Kerkorian, but kept the film library, the lot, and the buildings, which he still maintains on Clarington and Venice Boulevard, as well as a warehouse on Jefferson. In 1986 Turner sold the studio lot to Lorimar. The local citizens were saddened to see the historic sign removed from Stage Number 6. MGM Vice President Roger Mayer, who became president of Turner Entertainment, had worked with the city and the local historical society

to effect an historic sign ordinance.

The familiar sign, now protected by law, was moved across the street and placed atop the Filmland building, the new home of MGM. On June 11, 1987, studio CEO Lee Rich was joined by Gene Kelly and Culver City's Mayor Richard Brundo on a platform with a silky maned "Leo." As guests were treated to tunes from *That's Entertainment,* a spectacular 2 1/2-minute fireworks show sparked the lighting ceremony that brought the MGM trademark home again.

Lorimar, which already occupied office space on the studio lot, was shooting features and its most successful TV series, "Knots Landing" and "Dallas." Culver City homegrown Linda Gray starred as Sue Ellen opposite Larry Hagman in "Dallas." Lorimar put little into the facility, barely maintaining it. In 1988 the studio was experiencing financial difficulty, which precipitated a merger with Warner Brothers on January 1, 1989. Warner Brothers sold the historic studio lot to the Sony Corporation for Columbia Pictures Entertainment in January 1990. This marked the first time in 20 years that Columbia operated its own lot. Columbia's motion picture operations were comprised of two major studios, Columbia Pictures and Tri-Star Pictures. Columbia Senior Vice President of Finance and Administration Kenneth Williams unveiled the studio's 15-year plan for renovation of the facility. Williams and Vice President Barbara Cline are working with the City of Culver City on interim improvements as well as a comprehensive plan. Offices are being restored to house Columbia Chairman Peter Guber. On August 7, 1991, Sony's board of directors voted to change the corporate name Columbia Pictures Entertainment to Sony Pictures Entertainment. The operating companies retained their names. MGM/UA, across the street, was up for grabs. A deal with Quintec was in the works when the Australian company went bankrupt. Parretti's Pathe Communications closed a deal before the end of 1990 that will probably splinter MGM/UA beyond recognition.

In the early 1960s, before Kirk Kerkorian bought MGM and before redevelopment of the city, Culver City's schools peaked in population with more than 7,000 students in attendance from kindergarten through 12th grade. The Adult School grew, offering not only the opportunity for completion of high school, but also an independent learning center, ESL classes (English as a second language), and evening classes in everything from flower arranging with local master designer Michael Eskridge to estate planning or plumbing. The cost is minimal for senior citizens to encourage participation by a broad scope of the population.

By 1980 the district was experiencing declining enrollment, and, with the help of a facilities committee headed by Assistant Superintendent Tom Sanchez, a plan evolved for some schools to be closed and for the grades to be realigned. It was an emotional issue that was met with great opposition. In June 1981 El Marino and Linda Vista, two of Culver City's eight elementary schools, ceased operation. In 1983 it was necessary to close the doors of Betsy Ross and Washington

schools. The adjustment had one more component. Superintendent Dr. Curtis Rethmeyer remembers that the ninth graders became a part of a four-year high school, leaving just seventh and eighth graders in the junior high school for a year. The next year the sixth graders joined the seventh and eighth graders, and the junior high became a middle school (1983). The children of the early baby boomers are finally having children, and, as the elementary population grows, the reopening of one school is a possibility. Since the district has a growing Spanish Immersion Program, options for a new school include a magnet school. The four

schools that were closed are being leased. In 1979 Sunrise High School, which has been known as Culver Park since 1987, was established as an alternative high school at the El Marino site.

In the mid-1980s, after heated discussion, UCLA helped sponsor a youth health center to serve middle and high school students. The district also offers a children's center preschool and school-age child-care programs for before and after school at each elementary site. Child-care programs are also offered by the YMCA and the city.

Since Proposition 13 was passed in 1978, the funding base for the schools has changed. Monies are primarily directed out of the

Members of the 1990 Board of Education are pictured from left to right: Dr. Robert Knopf, Dr. Bess Drust, Linda Price, Julie Lugo Cerra, and Jim Quirarte. Courtesy, Julie Lugo Cerra

This 1954 aerial shows Hughes Aircraft (center) and Loyola Marymount University at the bottom. The community of West-chester is seen at center, right. Courtesy, Culver City Historical Society

state's general fund and are unstable at best. Because of the lack of control over funding, the school district had been afraid to enter into any long-range planning. Maintenance was cut, often until it could no longer be ignored. After the Board of Education declined to participate in the city's new civic center, the district was able to negotiate an amended contract with the Redevelopment Agency. The 1990 contract provided for $2.2 million for capital improvements and an annual stipend. A Strategic Planning Committee was established, with representation from the district, Board of Education, and community. A mission statement was adopted in 1990, and task forces have been established to work on goals.

While American history is a required subject in Culver City schools, local history is barely covered. So local residents rely on the

area's historical society to teach and preserve Culver City's heritage. Although there had been false starts in the past, a Culver City Historical Society was solidly founded in 1980. With pushes from old-timers such as Clarita Young and Frank McCann, plans were formulated and the incorporation papers were filed by attorney Paul Jacobs, a veteran city councilmember.

The society's first fund-raiser was a fashion show featuring some of the costumes Syd Kronenthal had rescued from the MGM auction. Local models wore the historic wardrobe items, and an impressive slide show served as a backdrop.

The society preserves the history of the area by offering lectures, historic tours, and exhibits. The society to date has marked eight historic sites: City Hall (9770 Culver

Dedicated in the 1980s as a 41-acre park, Culver Park is enjoyed not only by Little League teams, but also by the senior citizens softball team, seen here in practice. Photo by Amy Seidman-Tighe

LEFT: Members of the Culver City Historical Society gather for the dedication of Historic Site #1, the City Hall building. From left to right are: Dale Jones, Paul Netzel, Richard Alexander, Ron Perkins, Richard Brundo, Cathy Zermeno (then Historical Society president), Paul Jacobs, and Charles Lugo. Courtesy, Julie Lugo Cerra

Boulevard—1928), the Hull Building (the first hospital in the area—1925), St. Augustine's (the first church in the area—1887), Citizen Building (1929), Legion Building (1925), Main Street (1913), the studio at 9336 Washington Boulevard (1919), and the Lugo Ranch. The Native Daughters of the Golden West marked the site of the first studio in Culver City (10202 Washington Boulevard—1915), and the Sons of the Desert placed a marker near the Hal Roach Studio site (1919-1963).

Community support has been broad, with fund-raisers ranging from auctions to "A Celebration of the Movies," held at the studio where "Atlanta was burned" for *Gone With the Wind* 50 years before. A prime objective of the historical society is to establish a museum where the collection can be safely housed and appreciated by others.

And so, by 1992 the city would look back upon its early beginnings, the days when Indians sought higher ground to protect their camps, the festive and difficult times of land-grants, and Harry Culver's shaping of bean fields into "The Heart of Screenland."

6 *A Take!*

AS THE 1980S WERE FADING, CULVER CITY'S ELECTED OFFICIALS RESPONDED to some clearly emergent core issues. Since the 1960s the City Council had watched the rapid growth in Los Angeles County with concern. Traffic congestion was becoming paramount, and development pressures came to the forefront. Harry Culver's little city had grown from 1.2 to 5 square miles in a series of 37 annexations. The irregular border of the city presented post office and police problems.

The police department estimated a residential population of 40,000 added to commercial numbers of 320,000 to yield a policing population of 360,000 daily. Under the leadership of Police Chief Ted Cooke, the department has become very education oriented. With 117 officers, including 12 women, there are 132 earned degrees.

Non-sworn police personnel number 42. The police response time in Culver City is 12 minutes with emergencies at three minutes, which is attributed in part to having 71 percent of the force in the field. Although crime in Culver City has been on a down cycle since 1980, Cooke sees his biggest frustration a little broader, in that we have "gone from a nation of laws to a nation of lawyers." He points to a "bloated, time consuming, expensive judicial process" that inconveniences people who have already been victimized. He budgets for the DARE program in the schools to help students be drug free and uses asset-seizure money for predelinquency diversion.

The Culver City Fire Department grew from a few volunteers to a three-station department with a fine paramedic service. Fire Chief Michael Olson is most proud of the response time with emergency equipment—two to three minutes—which he points out "is almost unheard of in the state." He cites the high morale of the department and its esprit de corps as a contributing factor. In the last 15 years, the department has only added paramedics and one fire inspector. Frugal management has kept the number of personnel the same for the last 10 years. There are 71 sworn firefighters, and, with the clerical staff, the building department, and code enforcement and hazardous materials sections, the staff jumps to just more than 100. Olson, who has served as chief since 1985, views his department's great challenge as hazardous materials and toxic waste. In the next few years, an upgrading of computer equipment should provide batallion chiefs with the capability to access information on the scene with respect to hazardous materials and building layout.

The ethnic mix of the community changed completely over the years. The area, sparsely settled by transient Gabrielinos, yielded to the Spanish ranchos that evolved into a homogeneous community of English-speaking citizens. By 1990 a cultural mix turned Culver City into a microcosm of the real world. The schools, which had been all English-speaking in the early 1960s, had to adjust to 26 different languages spoken by its population, with 25 percent regarded by the school district as "limited English proficient." The ethnic picture changed to 30 percent Hispanic, 10 percent Black, 14 percent Asian, and 44 percent Caucasian. With these factors

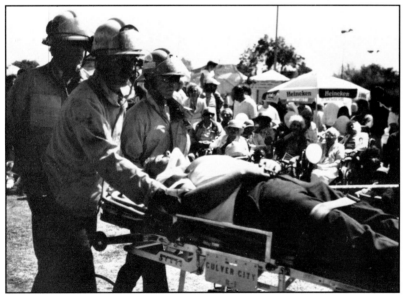

The Culver City Fire Department has come a long way since its volunteer-staffed days. Now the department has three stations and is fully equipped to handle all emergencies for the area. Here firefighters conduct a practice run for onlookers. Photo by Amy Seidman-Tighe

in mind, as well as rapid technological and economic changes, the need to maintain innovation and creativity in city management and "to make Culver City a superior city for community and business," the City Council authorized "Direction 21" on June 8, 1987. Paul A. Netzel, who made the motion to begin strategic planning, saw "the need for the council to act as the catalyst, to pull together a broad base of community support, to define a vision of the city 20 years hence."

Direction 21 boasted a steering committee of 56 members. Thirty-six were community representatives, including a participant from the Senior Citizens Association. The five councilmembers (Paul A. Jacobs, Paul A. Netzel, Richard Alexander, Jozelle Smith, and

Richard Brundo) sat on the committee with a representative from the Board of Education and one representative from each city commission (Planning, Civil Service, and Human Services and Park). The 10 City department heads were also members of the steering committee (Chief Administrative Officer Dale Jones, City Clerk Pauline Dolce, City Treasurer Lu Herrera, then Sue McCabe, Chief of Police Elwin "Ted" Cooke, Fire Chief Michael Olson, Municipal Services Director Gary Audet, Human Services Director Syd Kronenthal, Transportation Director Dave Ashcraft, Community Development Director Jody Hall-Esser, and City Attorney Joseph Pannone). After a six-week, well-advertised campaign for community representatives, the city received 120 applications. The selection process of the first 21 members was complete by the end of September that year. In April 1988 the City Council appointed another 15 representatives. The steering committee began to develop a vision of what they would like to see Culver City look like in the twenty-first century. The next phase was an environmental scan process in which there was a written and verbal analysis of key economic, social, and environmental factors that could impact the community. This gave way to the identification of key strategic issues and led to the creation of mission statements to guide the community as the issues were addressed. After two years of workshops, focus group meetings, and a citywide survey, the Direction 21 steering committee identified six strategic issue areas. Later development pointed to 26 ranked "Strategic Directions." In March 1989 the City Council adopted this series of issues and their corresponding mission statements: Strategic Issue: Government Financing Mission Statement: To provide a stable and predictable financial base to support current and future requirements.
Strategic Issue: City Appearance/Identity Mission Statement: To enhance the appearance of public and private property, encourage high-quality development and improve Culver City's regional identity as an

aesthetically desirable community.

Strategic Issue: Commercial/Residential Mix

Mission Statement: To ensure the high quality of life by promoting a viable mix of residential/commercial/industrial development that provides a strong economic base for both city services and successful business operations.

Strategic Issue: Transportation/ Traffic

Mission Statement: To develop improved transportation and traffic systems to move the public in a convenient, efficient, and safe manner.

Strategic Issue: Education

Mission Statement: To work cooperatively with school systems to develop and promote high-quality education.

Strategic Issue: Recreation/Culture/ Entertainment

Mission Statement: To provide and encourage the development of recreational, cultural, and entertainment facilities and programs to enhance the quality of life in Culver City.

Within these issues were contained certain mandates. The "no-growth" or "slow-growth" attitude throughout the state was apparent with a strong discouragement of "mini-malls and fast food establishments." On the other hand, the message was somewhat mixed with a strong directive to continue the work of the Redevelopment Agency. Improved traffic flow ranked high to protect residents. Communication rose to the surface as a high priority, as citizens wanted to see themselves as informed members of the business and residential communities. Recreation and cultural activities received strong encouragement as did a tying of activities to the city's film industry heritage.

The city faced major changes. The new civic center was designed. A charette process in 1991 provided a vision for the redevelopment of "downtown." The school district decided to upgrade its district office on its own site. The Culver Municipal Court was bursting its seams, but could not afford to become a part of the new civic center. Chief Administrative Officer H. Dale Jones decided to retire at the end of 1991. Jones, a young man who

These construction workers lay the foundation for the Fox Hills Mall. Ernest Hahn, Inc., was the co-developer and contractor for the 45-acre shopping mall. Courtesy, Culver City Historical Society

was raised in Masonic orphanages, had found a comfortable home in Culver City and had served as the chief administrator since 1969. He gained the reputation for becoming one of the longest-standing CAO's in the country. He was proud of the working relationship/ joint powers agreement between the city and the school district. Civic-minded Dale Jones' easy manner and ability to get along with all of the councils he served under left big shoes to fill.

The political climate of the city was also stormy. Assemblywoman Gwen Moore sent out a last-minute campaign mailer to support three city council candidates in 1988: favorite son Paul Jacobs and challenger Steven Gourley as well as Dr. James Boulgarides (who had

served years before). The net result was a defeat for incumbents Paul Netzel and Richard Brundo. Some viewed the election as a result of "outside interference," others as a Democratic victory in a nonpartisan election. Nonetheless, the city became divided, and the 1990 election was evidence of stormy waters again. A height-limit initiative called Measure I narrowly defeated the council offering, Measure II, but the grass-roots candidate, Tom Hammons, was defeated by a young conservative "homegrown" electrical contractor named Michael Balkman.

About the same time the city began its long-range planning, the Culver City Unified School District established a Strategic Planning Committee. The process began in the spring of 1988, with a group selected to represent a broad spectrum of the community. Superintendent Dr. Curtis Rethmeyer, with the aid of county consultants, led the process with members Jim Carr, Bess Doerr (teacher—CC Middle School), Dr. Bess Drust (Board of Education), LeRoy Hale (head custodian—La Ballona School), Joy Jacobs (district communication specialist), Dr. Anita Johnson (principal—Culver Park High School), Diane Kaiser (teacher—CC High School), Jim Lang (retired principal representing the community), G. James Quirarte (Board of Education), Kelley Roberts (teacher—Farragut School), and Diane Wallace (principal—La Ballona School). By January 1990 a mission statement and 13 prioritized goals were adopted by the Culver City Board of Education. The mission statement was printed, framed, and now hangs in the district office and on all school sites as a reminder of the district's goals: "The mission of the Culver City Unified School District is to provide our diverse population with a stimulating lifelong learning environment which fosters the maximum development of responsible, productive members of society. This will be accomplished through:
- a foundation of basic skills
- a broad-based curriculum
- accountability of results
- utilization of community resources

- input regarding decisions from students, staff, parents, and community members
- support systems for all students and staff
- safe and secure facilities
- valid learning programs and strategies
- sound fiscal policies"

Because of the cost factor, only the first seven goals were addressed by task forces immediately. They involved curriculum, safe and secure environment, compensation, facilities, shared decision-making, communication, and high school restructuring. The process was designed to be ongoing, but early action included the hiring of a security manager, a communication specialist, a proposed model district crisis and rumor control plan, and a parcel tax steering committee.

As the city of Culver City was reaching its 75th anniversary in 1992, some, like Community Development Director Jody Hall-Esser, saw it "at a crossroads," others as an oasis in an urban metropolis. Redevelopment was an ongoing reality. The major movie studios were reduced to the two. The Culver Studios was newly renovated, and Sony Pictures Entertainment, which owned both, was settling in at Thomas Ince's first studio and came home to Culver City with a 15-year comprehensive plan, again proving that Culver City is indeed "The Heart of Screenland."

ABOVE: The Culver Studios boasts beautifully landscaped grounds. Photo by Larry Molmud

FACING PAGE, TOP: Fiesta La Ballona, as it was originally called, was conceived as a week-long celebration of the area's Spanish heritage. It ran for 13 consecutive years, beginning in 1951, and was later reinstated in the 1980s as the Festival of the People. Seen in this picture is a Machado descendant (in the back seat) and Clarita Young. In the front seat is Charles Lugo with granddaughter Michele Cerra. Courtesy, Julie Lugo Cerra

FACING PAGE, BOTTOM: Before the marina was built, La Ballona Creek entered directly into the ocean without any obstruction. Courtesy, Culver City Historical Society

7 Partners in Progress

ON JULY 25, 1913, AT THE CALIFORNIA CLUB IN LOS ANGELES, HARRY Culver, of the newly formed Culver Investment Company, announced his plans for a city that would be a balanced residential/commercial community. Within a year of this announcement, Culver City had, among other ventures, a grocery store, a bank, a newspaper, and a real estate sales force of 150. Trees were planted, a lighting system was designed, and streets were paved.

MGM's musical Take Me Out To The Ball Game *starred Frank Sinatra and Gene Kelly. The 1949 sensation also starred the red-headed Esther Williams. ©1949 Turner Entertainment Co. All Rights Reserved*

As Harry Culver's plans for development moved forward, he witnessed the filming of a movie in 1915 at La Ballona Creek. His intrigue with the movie industry helped him convince Thomas Ince to move from his Inceville studio north of Santa Monica to prime property on Washington Boulevard. This was to be the first of Culver City's three major motion picture studios, which would provide for its sound economic base.

The Board of Supervisors filed Culver City's articles of incorporation with the Secretary of State on September 20, 1917. It was official. Harry Culver's dream had come true.

Today the city that began as a dream continues to grow and prosper. Much of the credit for this growth and success belongs to the organizations whose stories appear on the following pages. Their support of this important literary and civic project is a reflection of their pride in Culver City's progress.

Culver City Chamber Of Commerce

Its mission statement is clear and to the point: "To create and maintain a favorable business climate and an attractive area in which to live and do business." The Culver City Chamber of Commerce, like the community it represents, strives for a balance between good living and vital commerce to ensure a bright future.

With a population of some 40,000 persons, 18,000 residential units, and 4,000 business sites, Culver City has maintained its "small-town identity within the metropolis," according to chamber president Steven J. Rose. "There is an independent spirit here, a great sense of ownership that is reflected in our chamber's approach."

The chamber has 850 members comprising leading businesses, professionals, and interested individuals who work together for the common good. The mix includes prominent industries such as electronics, computer services, motion pictures, and aircraft manufacturing, as well as lawyers, realtors, and retailers.

In strong support of free enterprise and community self-reliance, the chamber has a solid voluntary organization that works effectively through a number of committees.

Legislative involvement is a primary committee activity on local, state, and national levels, with participants keeping tabs on every issue that affects local businesses and working with the chamber's board of directors for best results.

"We are both the voice of the business community and a public relations arm of the city," Rose emphasizes.

The chamber dates back to 1917 when it was formed as a businessman's association the same year the city was incorporated. Historically, chamber leadership has been a major force in keeping property costs and taxes equitable. Indeed, many past chamber chairpersons have gone on to city government.

For the public, the chamber provides a daily information source, and periodic economic profiles on growth and trends.

For its members, the chamber offers a multitude of benefits: marketing information, retail promotions programs, small-business management seminars, networking opportunities, and a referral service. There is an annual city business expo at which member businesses display their goods and services, an annual Secretary Day event for 300 that sells out each time, an annual golf tournament, and other social events. Special goodwill ambassadors, called "Los Caballeros," attend ground breakings, grand openings, and help plan and work annual fundraisers. Ongoing awards programs recognize local businesses, and new members have a "Breakfast Club" to make them feel at home.

It is a small-town orientation with big-city successes, Rose points out. "We vigorously support charitable efforts in youth and education—the YMCA, Little League, Scouting, and AYSO Soccer. We have a scholarship program, a popular teacher-of-the-year award, and a busy speakers' bureau. Belonging to the chamber is like buying a share of stock in the community's future."

1991-92 Board of Directors

Executive Committee
Chairman of the Board
Michael Fate, Esq. .... Law Offices of Michael Fate
Vice Chair/Membership Services
Bill Silvestre .... Eagle Group
Vice Chair/Governmental Relations
Stephen Hadland .... Coast Media
Vice Chair/Community & Economic Services
Gordon Fell .... Gordon Fell, CPA
Vice Chair/CFO
Wendy Miller .... Wendy Miller, CPA
Member-at-Large
Gale Campbell .... AFP Group
President
Steven J. Rose
Barbara Cline .... Sony Pictures Entertainment
Diane Carter ....Sietsema Communications
Dan Cohen .... The Kitchen Store
Bob Duitsman .... Duitsman & Hughes
Earl Eskridge .... Culver Center Flower
George Fierro ....Culver Palms Ymca
Tim Giarraffa..20th Century Security Systems
Alan Goldman .... Culver City Industrial Hardware
Lee Jordan .... Lee Jordan & Associates
Pierre Joujon-Roche .... King's Hallmark
Carol Mallen .... Filmcorp
John Newhouse .... Culver National Bank
Ron Phelps .... Brotman Medical Center
Cy Pierce, CPA .... An Accountancy Corp
Judy Potik .... Horticultural Management
Jim Quirarte .... Gus Music
Curtis Reis .... Alliance Bank
Bob Steinberg .... Culver City Educational Foundation
Helen Vaughn .... Vaughn Enterprises
Rita Zide .... Roll 'n Rye Restaurant

Alliance Bank

True to its name, Alliance Bank builds its professional reputation on its bond with customers.

Entrepreneurial in spirit, the community bank aims primarily to serve small businesses, typically up to $10-million in revenues; professionals like lawyers, architects, and certified public accountants; and executives of any size business with interests separate from their corporate banking programs.

The nature of the bank has changed some since its early days (it was founded in 1980) to fit new customer needs " . . . like hand in glove," according to chairman and president Curtis S. Reis. "We often serve in effect as unpaid financial officers for our small business clients, counseling them when they are faced with important economic decisions. Being responsive to customers is our greatest asset, the real value-added we can offer."

To do this, employees must develop a close working relationship with those who entrust the bank with their major deposit and credit business. Alliance has met the challenge

by becoming compact and streamlined. Ninety percent of Alliance Bank's staff can focus on customer service because much of the operational work—such as data processing, legal, auditing, even some marketing—is done off-site by specialists. Bank officials say the process is cost-effective, brings fresh suggestions into the system, encourages prompt decisions on transactions, and avoids duplication of effort.

"It has also allowed us to upgrade employees' positions and give them an opportunity to learn a number of banking functions," adds Reis, a great believer in education and cross-training who serves not only as chief executive but as " . . . the senior marketing person and the other senior lending officer. I enjoy getting involved in every aspect of the business, especially the customer contact."

Reis, who served as senior vice president of Crocker National Bank before he joined the publicly held Alliance in 1986, is one of nine officers at the bank whose accumulated experience adds up to more than 200 years.

Curtis S. Reis, chairman and president of Alliance Bank.

Alliance Bank's physical plant has changed dramatically since its May 1980 opening in a temporary modular building. In February 1985 the bank moved into its current headquarters at 100 Corporate Pointe, the commercial business park on Slauson in the Fox Hills developed by Bramalea Limited of Canada. Alliance Bank's bright, contemporary quarters occupy over 11,000 square feet on the ground floor of a three-story low-rise—almost double its former space.

What are its special services for the 1990s? Prime among them is a mortgage-loan source, in which the bank shops the national market for its busy customers. Active, ongoing community involvement is part of the mix, with annual fair sponsorships and periodic newsletters for the community, small-business seminar presentations designed to help owners more effectively manage and grow, and staff volunteerism for needy groups—all part of the bank's energetic and enthusiastic posture in Culver City's thriving economy.

Alliance Bank

Sony Pictures Studios

Fantasy becomes reality inside the walls of Sony Pictures Studios in Culver City. Here the Munchkins romped along the Yellow Brick Road that stretched from Stage 27 across Main Street to Stage 15. Here J.R. Ewing and his clan fought—and loved—their way around Southfork Ranch house exteriors and pool, recreated for the long-running television series on Stage 23. Here *Hook* sailed his way into the modern-day film version of Peter Pan on a massive sound stage containing a full-sized ship last summer.

But today's 44.7-acre studio lot is neither Oz nor Never-Never Land, although it recently resembled the latter. It is a working entertainment production facility for a diverse number of efforts including motion pictures, television shows, and videos that reach a worldwide audience. As part of Sony Pictures Entertainment, Inc. (SPE), the studios play a major role in the global entertainment marketplace.

Sony Pictures Studios, bounded by Washington Boulevard on the north, Culver Boulevard on the south, Madison Avenue on the east, and Overland Avenue on the west, has been a Culver City landmark since 1916.

The entrance to Columbia on Gower Street's "Poverty Row."

The Thalberg Building, recognized as a landmark structure by the city, was constructed in the 1930s as the studio's administration facility and named in memory of MGM's young genius Irving Thalberg, who was head of production. Thalberg was married to actress Norma Shearer. Photo by Derek Raff

Under present ownership by its parent Sony Corporation, which acquired SPE in November 1989 and took ownership of the studios in January 1990, the facility is fast becoming a premier location for some of the most innovative and sophisticated technology in the industry. Through a phased-in transition, the studios are combining Sony's world renowned hardware with SPE's acclaimed software to offer the creative community an ongoing state-of-the-art approach to the filmed entertainment business.

The Sony/SPE plan is to test the limits continuously in both sight and sound film production techniques by mingling newly developed computer and video technologies. Sony has been working on fresh ways to cross-pollinate media—adapting music and video to tapes, discs, and computers—for some time. It is light years away from Columbia's first "talkie," made in 1929.

SPE, now headquartered on its new Sony Pictures Studios lot, was officially acquired by Sony USA, Inc., a subsidiary of the Sony Corporation. The Sony/SPE combination as a large diversified company is a formidable industry force in television programming, distribution and syndication,

theatrical exhibition, and home video, as well as film production. It does business in 100 countries worldwide—primarily in theatrical and TV distribution, and in a joint venture through Columbia Tri Star international videos. Within SPE, motion picture operations are comprised of two major studios: Columbia Pictures and TriStar Pictures.

Today the company employs more than 3,000 people, mostly at West Coast Headquarters on the Sony Pictures lot in Culver City and at Studio Plaza in Burbank. (Some 1,000 are on the Culver City lot daily to support Columbia, TriStar, and other film companies who work here.)

The lot has a rich history of its own—a story within the Columbia story. It was first known as the Ince/Triangle Studios when it was established in 1916. The land and the financing were supplied by Harry Culver and supervised by pioneer film maker Thomas Ince. In 1918, when the Ince/Triangle Studios went bankrupt, the property was sold to Goldwyn Pictures.

The lot's history reflects much of the industry's history. It became part of the Goldwyn/Metro merger in 1923, then the Goldwyn, Metro, and Louis B. Mayer merger that formed Metro Goldwyn Mayer (MGM) Studios in 1924.

Eventually the studios encompassed 180 acres with six lots. Lot 1, on 44.77 acres and all that remains of the original property or studio (it was six parcels) was used then—as now—for primary buildings, sound stages, scene docks, and rehearsal halls, among other things. The other lots were used mainly for outdoor sets such as cities, towns, villages, lakes, and jungles. But yesterday's fantasy jungles have been replaced by today's Culver City shops, businesses, and housing.

On a normal working day, the huge lot had more than 5,000 employees, not including production people, and as many as 100,000 extras at one time. The chariot scenes for the original *Ben Hur* were constructed on empty land near Venice and La Cienega.

Louis B. Mayer's first office on Lot 1 was in the Harlow Building. (Most of the early structures are named for venerable stars: Jean Harlow, Joan Crawford, Myrna Loy, Fred Astaire, Judy Garland, and Cary Grant, to name a few.) Mayer's office walls were covered in white leather, and had silent floor switches near his desk to summon various aides. His office was later moved to the now-landmark Thalberg Building, named for Irving Thalberg, the MGM executive known for his genius in steering product selection.

Throughout its tenure, the studio

The popular Three Stooges movies were filmed at Columbia. Courtesy of Columbia Pictures. ©1939, Renewed 1967, Columbia Pictures Industries, Inc. All Rights Reserved

lot has seen a prodigious number of stars, productions, and technologies thrive as a result of the creative genius and collective energy expressed here. That history amazingly parallels Columbia's own background.

Spanning three-quarters of a century, Columbia's roots can be traced back to 1919 when three men—Harry and Jack Cohn and Joe Brandt—formed a partnership to produce low-budget shorts and featurettes which were modest but successful. They called the company CBC Film Sales, for Cohn-Brandt-Cohn (in the trade it was dubbed "Corned-Beef-and-Cabbage").

CBC got off to a near-disastrous start and almost went bankrupt when a director they hired in Hollywood pocketed most of the budget and produced several movie shorts that were unshowable. The trio decided Harry should be on the West Coast to oversee their next venture.

With Harry in California and Jack and Joe in New York, the partners built the resources to produce their first feature film. Released in 1922, the film was so successful it convinced the men

Clark Gable and Claudette Colbert starred in Columbia's first Academy Award-winning movie, Frank Capra's It Happened One Night. *Courtesy of Columbia Pictures. ©1934, Renewed 1962, Columbia Pictures Industries, Inc. All Rights Reserved*

to pursue a much grander approach to film production. In all, 10 full-length features were produced between August 1922 and December 1923. Despite its success, however, the company was still not a giant in the industry, and the old nickname of "Corned-Beef-and-Cabbage" popped up to haunt its proud owners. As a result, in January 1924 the humble CBC became the nobler Columbia Pictures Corporation. Its offices continued in New York, with leased space in Hollywood.

At first Harry Cohn set up a modest shop, in keeping with the company's fledgling products. The company rented an office in Hollywood among the small maverick outfits around Gower Street and Sunset Boulevard, an area known as "Poverty Row." But as the company continued to grow and expand, Harry purchased a small studio nearby in 1926. The tiny lot grew through added acreage over the next decades to accommodate Columbia's growth.

Brothers Harry and Jack are said to have had a lifelong sibling rivalry that spurred them to constant one-upmanship, and therefore great accomplishments. Joe Brandt was the man in the middle.

One year after Harry bought the company's own studio, Frank Capra came on board. He proved to be the studio's single greatest asset, for during his 12 years with Columbia his work was a significant factor in the company's rise to major studio status.

His directing talents became legendary, contributing to a number of "firsts" for Columbia. None was greater, however, than Columbia's first Academy Award for the 1934 Capra film *It Happened One Night*. In fact, the picture swept five top awards and put the studio on the map.

Capra continued to direct other films that were destined to become classics, such as *Mr. Smith Goes To Washington*, while Harry led the company into prosperity during the 1930s and 1940s. It is said that during the Depression years the company barely slowed down. Still on Gower Street, the studio had spilled over its capacity.

Clearly it needed more space, so in 1935 the company acquired additional acreage in Burbank, called "the Ranch," for location filming. But it had also kept the Poverty Row location, gradually absorbing it rather than leaving it.

It was during the 1940s that Columbia produced its biggest grossing film to date at that time: *The Jolson Story*. Coupled with several other hits, the picture gave the Studios its most profitable decade since its inception, topped off in 1949 with another Best Picture Oscar for *All the King's Men*.

From the mid-1950s onward Columbia began to distribute movies that were not made "in-house," yet the films figure as an integral part of the company's history because of the Studio's creative and financial

ABOVE: The setup for shooting a movie scene inside the lot, on "A" Street.

RIGHT: Klieg lights shine on one of the Loews theaters.

involvement. The approach ushered in a new era in the business of the film industry.

Hollywood in the 1950s was mostly in turbulence, following the boom years of the 1940s. Television, for many studios, posed a major threat, with cinema attendances dropping drastically. But Columbia chose to be a pioneer in its evolution and development through a new subsidiary—Screen Gems, which produced television shows. Under Jack Cohn's son Ralph, Screen Gems also distributed theatrical motion pictures, an important step toward creating what is now one of the most extensive television and film libraries in the industry.

Both the Cohn brothers died in the late 1950s, and there was a mood of uncertainty reflected in the studio's product for a time. It was the end of an era, but Cohn associates ultimately moved the company into the next decade with continuity. There were

three more Oscar winning successes to prove it: *From Here to Eternity* in 1953, *On the Waterfront* in 1954, and *The Bridge on the River Kwai* in 1957.

Viewers in the 1960s wanted youth-oriented themes, so Columbia brought along movies like *Georgy Girl* and *To Sir With Love,* and still more Oscar winners. Among them: *Lawrence of Arabia* in 1962 and *A Man For All Seasons* in 1966. (Columbia opened its own production office in England in 1965, and its British-made hits contributed to financial solvency in changing economic times.)

The 1960s also saw the rise of independent producers who rented space on the Columbia lot. The most suc-

cessful was *Lawrence of Arabia*'s Sam Spiegel, who brought profit and prestige with him.

Columbia's television business took the lead again in the 1970s, when the company combined its television operations into Columbia Pictures Television and innovated, among other formats, the first miniseries ("QB VII") and made-for-TV movies.

In 1972 the company moved everything to Burbank, and merged its real estate holdings with Warner Communications to form The Burbank Studios, a facility they were to share for 18 years. By late 1972, all vestiges of the studio's Poverty Row association had been removed. The British connection also ended, after several commercial disasters produced there offset domestic successes like *Bob and Carol and Ted and Alice* and *Five Easy Pieces.* Fortunately, at that same time, several profitable Barbra Streisand hits were made, including *The Way We Were* and *Funny Lady.*

To close out the decade, the studio embarked on a highly profitable period again, with such successful films as *Close Encounters of the Third Kind, Shampoo, Taxi Driver, Midnight Express,* and *Kramer vs. Kramer,* which won an Oscar in 1979.

The fast-moving 1980s were also a decade of growth and change for Columbia. Corporate changes led to its purchase by The Coca-Cola Company in 1982, with a cash and stock deal valued at between $700- and $800-million.

Columbia extended its entertainment activities to other areas such as home video, and in 1986 acquired Merv Griffin Enterprises, producer of the top two television game shows, *Wheel of Fortune* and *Jeopardy!* During this period the Studios had some of its

ABOVE: The famed studio "east gate," through which passed more stars than were in the heavens. The commissary, pictured just inside the gate, is where Mrs. Louis B. Mayer taught the chef to make her studio chief husband's favorite matzo ball soup. Photo by Derek Raff

RIGHT: Steven Spielberg came to Culver City to make Hook. *The TriStar release stars Dustin Hoffman as Captain Hook, Robin Williams as Peter Pan, and Julia Roberts as Tinkerbell in what promises to become a family classic.*

biggest hits in *Tootsie, Ghostbusters,* and *Ghandi,* which won Best Picture in 1982.

On a parallel track, HBO and CBS joined together in 1983 to form the first new major motion picture studio in decades—TriStar Pictures. TriStar achieved the fastest growth from start-up to major studio in the industry's history, with wide-ranging successes in film production and distribution such as *Peggy Sue Got Married, The Natural,* and *Rambo: First Blood Part II.*

In 1986 TriStar entered the theatrical exhibition business by purchasing the Loews theater circuit. The oldest, and one of the six largest exhibition circuits in the United States, Loews operates some 850 motion picture screens in 16 states and has a significant presence in most major metropolitan areas east of the Mississippi River.

In late 1987 Coca-Cola's Entertainment Business Sector and TriStar Pictures combined to form the publicly held Columbia Pictures Entertainment, now an international organization.

Rounding out the 1980s, Columbia Pictures garnered the company's twelfth Best Picture Oscar for *The Last Emperor* (in 1988), and achieved many other noteworthy box office successes, *Ghostbusters II* and *Steel Magnolias* among them. By this time it had also amassed an enormous film library of 3,000 motion pictures. It is one of the most comprehensive collections anywhere, with many classics, commercial successes, and critically acclaimed films.

When Sony purchased Columbia in 1989 it created a whole new range of opportunities. One of the greatest benefits to the company is full control of its own studio facility for the first time in 20 years. Now, through a careful renovation that maintains the integrity of the lot's history—especially the Art Deco architecture of the 1930s—but upgrades existing facilities, SPE is making a major commitment to the future of the Culver City property. Its significant investment puts less emphasis on large industrial-type space and more on creative and administrative space.

For example, the landmark Thalberg Building, which reflects movie-making's Golden Era, continues as the lot's anchor, while an important studio crafts center and new stages will be added.

The plan brings currently underutilized land areas on the lot into full use, and reclaims and consolidates existing facilities into more efficient modern structures, all set in a campus-like environment.

Driven by technological advances and the demands of increasingly sophisticated world markets, the SPE/Sony Pictures Studios renovation will customize facilities for the most advanced technologies and technical innovations. In audio, for example, production specialists are touting digital sound for editing and scoring a film—of interest to virtually every major studio. Digital sound, they say, makes conventional methods sound primitive by comparison.

With the introduction of high-definition technologies for motion pictures and television, SPE/Sony is exploring new ways to offer such capabilities to the creative community to present worldwide audiences with a whole new era of cinematic accomplishment.

The Sony Pictures Entertainment of the 1990s is a company with fully revitalized motion picture development, production, and distribution capabilities. Under the leadership of chairman and chief executive officer Peter Guber, SPE has surged to first place at the domestic box office with such major hits as *Postcards From The Edge, Misery, Awakenings,* and two of 1991's biggest hits: *Terminator 2: Judgement Day* and *City Slickers.*

SPE featured a powerful line-up of feature films for Christmas 1991 and beyond, including Steven Spielberg's *Hook,* starring Robin Williams, Dustin Hoffman, and Julia Roberts; Barry Levinson's *Bugsy,* featuring Warren Beatty and Annette Bening; Barbra Streisand's *Prince of Tides,* starring Streisand and Nick Nolte; Francis Ford Coppola's *Dracula,* starring Gary Oldman, Winona Ryder, and Anthony Hopkins and shot almost entirely on the Sony Pictures lot; and Penny Marshall's *A League Of their Own,* starring Tom Hanks, Madonna, and Geena Davis.

During the past two years SPE has also attracted a constellation of some of the greatest creative forces in the industry, including Jim Brooks, Steven Spielberg, Francis Ford Coppola, Michael Jackson, Barry Levinson, Penny Marshall, Danny DeVito, David and Jerry Zucker, Woody Allen, Arnold Schwarzenegger, and Martin Scorsese.

Although SPE is often perceived

ABOVE: Dustin Hoffman and Jessica Lange starred in Tootsie, *one of Columbia"s biggest hits. Courtesy of Columbia Pictures. ©1982, Columbia Pictures Industries, Inc. All Rights Reserved*

LEFT: Robert Redford in The Natural, *a major TriStar picture of the 1980s.*

mostly as a motion picture company, it also has a number of major TV shows to its credit as well. Its television operations are a major industry force in current prime time, daytime, and syndicated programming and distribution, with particular strength in half-hour comedies. Three major prime-time series—"Who's the Boss" (ABC), "Designing Women" (CBS), and "Married With Children" (FOX)—have recently been licensed into syndication for some of the top prices in industry history.

In fact, the entire television syndication list is long and impressive: 25,000 episodes of 270 different series, including a number of classics, like *The Three Stooges, Route 66, Maude, The Jeffersons, Charlie's Angels, Starsky and Hutch,* and *All in the Family.*

Top talent translates to top titles, of course, but not only for SPE's own distribution. The company entered a major agreement for the international theatrical distribution of all Orion films worldwide. With its strong network in place, the company recently formed Columbia TriStar International Releasing Corporation, a new group that combines CPE's international theatrical, international television, worldwide home video, pay television, and select ancillary operations under one umbrella.

SPE intends to continue strengthening and expanding its business, further developing a global entertainment company that sets the stage for the evolution of even more innovative entertainment ahead. It is the company's answer to a worldwide trend—rising living standards and increased leisure time—just waiting to be claimed.

The Quirarte Family

Well-known Culver City residents Gus and Bertha Quirarte have had their share of honors in recent years for community service: Gus was named as "Citizen of the Year" by both the chamber of commerce and board of realtors, and Bertha as "Woman of the Year" by the Soroptimist Club, to name only a few.

But the Quirartes have said the honor was all theirs, being able to give something back to the city that has been home for almost a half-century. Here, their business—Gus' Music—and their children—Jimmy and Sandy—flourished.

The Quirartes came to Culver City by way of Mexico and Los Angeles. Gus (Gonzalo) Quirarte was born in Torreon, Cohiala, Mexico, on February 19, 1912, one of eight children.

Bertha Quirarte

He came to the U.S. in 1925 (by way of Texas in a covered wagon) and lived in Boyle Heights, later graduating from Lincoln High. His father was a conductor for the Mexican Railroad during unstable political times. Gus, named for his father, left to avoid the revolutions.

Bertha was born Carolina Bertha De Avila in Chihuahua, Mexico, on March 29, 1916, one of seven children. She came to Los Angeles in 1927, when her father left his rancho to seek a better environment for his family. (He had been a stable boy for Emperor Maximilian—who just before his execution gave young De Avila 12 horses, which launched him

Gus Quirarte

in a ranching career.)

Gus and Bertha met at the Club Imperial, a social club in Los Angeles, and were married on November 25, 1938. Gus worked in his family's laundry service, where each of the seven sons had his own truck. Three years later Gus and Bertha bought their first Culver City home.

When World War II broke out, Gus left to serve as a radio instructor in the Army Air Force in 1942. Bertha moved back with her parents, then joined him in Idaho several posts later. There, on June 21, 1945, son Jimmy (Gonzalo James) was born.

In 1946 they moved back to Culver City, and Gus went to work for a com-

pany that serviced coin-operated phonographs—jukeboxes. He started his own business in 1950, two years after their daughter Sandy was born.

Throughout the 1960s and 1970s the Quirarte's civic work burgeoned. Gus assumed leadership roles in the Pony and Colt leagues, Pop Warner football, the Lions Club (he was "Lion of the Year" in 1961-1962), Elks, Amvets, American Legion, Moose, and other organizations. In the mid-1970s he became a parks and recreation commissioner.

Bertha was a Girl Scout leader and den mother, and active in the Women's Club, Las Amigas, Culver City Guidance Clinic Guild, and the West Los Angeles College Advisory Board. Both Quirartes were honored with life memberships in the Farragut School PTA. And both enjoyed dancing and entertaining. It was not unusual for Bertha to prepare 100 chile rellenos dinners for charity.

Gus sold the business to his son in 1974, but was "recalled" a year later to provide a valuable service for the next 12 years. Son Jimmy married and raised his two sons in Culver City, where all three graduated from Culver High. Jimmy, like his parents, is committed to community service, serving in the Lions Club and as a member of the Culver City Board of Education. Sandy Quirarte married her high school sweetheart, Lance Cutler, and moved to Sonoma, where they raised a daughter.

In 1988 the Quirarte children and grandchildren joined together to honor Gus and Bertha on their 50th anniversary.

Culver National Bank

With a strong emphasis on friendly service and the belief that every bank customer is an important client, Culver National Bank has proven that quality financial services combined with a neighborly approach produce a loyal clientele.

"We serve people, not numbers. It's that simple," states founder and chairman of the board George Newhouse.

The bank was formed in 1984 to meet the local banking needs made evident by extensive market research which showed that small- to medium-sized businesses and individuals would welcome a personalized approach.

Located at 5399 Sepulveda, near Slauson, the bank generally serves clientele within a three-mile radius.

George Newhouse and president John Newhouse comprise the father-and-son management team that today oversees $50 million in assets. They are joined by a board of directors with roots in the Culver City area, well-known businesspersons who are highly visible in civic activities, as George and John are. The Newhouses have been officers or directors of the Exchange Club of Culver City, the Lions Club, the Chamber of Commerce, and the Culver/Palms YMCA.

Culver National Bank directors (left to right) are: June C. Malone, Bernard Pollock, William R. Fecho, Harrison F. Betts, George R. Newhouse, John R. Newhouse, Vernon Larsen, Roy M. Good, Dan Patacchia, and Earl S. Eskridge.

The elder Newhouse brought 27 years of savings and loan experience, and many of his former customers, to CNB. He had begun his banking career in another metropolis: Pittsburgh, Pennsylvania. He was lured to Southern California in 1945 after his military service was over, married his Santa Barbara-born wife, and began to build an early career in real estate lending and appraising.

In the mid-1950s Newhouse spearheaded the start of a substantial savings and loan organization, and helped fuel its growth until his attempt at retirement in 1982. "But retirement wasn't for me," Newhouse says, shaking his head. In less than a year and a half he headed a list of dedicated community leaders and local stockholders who created the much-needed local bank.

John Newhouse entered banking in 1978 after he graduated from the University of Southern California. As an auditor, then branch manager in the savings and loan industry, he was instrumental in founding CNB with his father. In April 1989 he was named president and elected to a seat on the bank's board of directors.

CNB, characterized by its manage-

John R. Newhouse, president (left) and George R. Newhouse, chairman of the board.

ment as strong in reserves and steady in its progressive development, concentrates its loan program on consumer and commercial lending. Its services are the same as major banks, John Newhouse notes, ". . . except we pride ourselves on quality, not quantity, through friendliness and efficiency."

A strength: the "WAIT-LESS" service concept, which is directed toward processing loan applications and making loan decisions faster, as well as simply shortening the time spent in line to make a deposit.

Staff longevity also creates the family atmosphere that CNB's founders sought. Because CNB has a strong recruiting program in the local schools, and a policy to promote from within, the bank has engendered a high degree of employee loyalty. Even the bank's decor is geared toward a homey "living room" feeling.

"People who live in Culver City have a deep sense of community," says George Newhouse. "We're like an island in the big sea of metropolitan L.A., with our own identity—and proud of it."

Roll N' Rye Restaurant

Perhaps the best lessons David and Bella Zide taught their three children were how to love people, live life to the fullest, and laugh a lot.

Now Rita Zide practices her parents' philosophy in her thriving restaurant and delicatessen, the Roll N' Rye, at 10990 Jefferson Boulevard. Her outstanding menu, full of savory foods and baked goods prepared on the premises, is available in the 140-seat, full-service restaurant, through take-out orders, and by specialized catering within a 20-mile radius. The Roll N' Rye has a large following, both on-site and served by its mobile van.

Today Rita blends her contemporary approach to the business with her appreciation for the historical, recognizing Culver City's changes since the restaurant opened here in 1963, and her mindfulness of her parents' wisdom regarding serving the public.

In dedicating this article to her parents, Rita remembers her late father David: "I miss him a lot, and I miss his advice. Mentors are fine but they are

Rita Zide at the original Culver City location a few weeks before demolition.

not like a parent. My dad was tough but fair." Of her mother Bella, now living in the San Fernando Valley, she says, "My mother was one of the best hostesses ever. She's very sweet. In the restaurant she always had a smile, but was a taskmaster in her own right, keeping everything flowing."

Over the years the Zides accumulated many outstanding recipes, and a reputation for making all their delicious entrees and much of their baked goods fresh on the premises. Nothing comes out of a can here. To fill its popular turkey sandwiches, the Roll N' Rye kitchen cooks 25 to 30 turkey breasts each day. To fill its legendary combination "Sky-high" sandwich, cooks pile not only turkey breast, but pastrami, roast beef, ham, tomato, and Thousand Island dressing on a Kaiser roll.

There are the typically hearty deli selections like homemade cheese

blintzes and stuffed cabbage; the assorted desserts like German chocolate cake and cheesecake. For lunch or dinner, there are the savory-but-good-for-you chicken dishes, with full-meal trimmings, and for the health-conscious, there are salads and vegetables.

Both David and Bella Zide emigrated from Europe, but a year apart—in 1915 and 1916. Both came to New York, then Chicago where they met and married. In the late 1930s they came to California and began their business and their family.

Rita and her older brothers Sol and Abe grew up with a healthy mix of sibling rivalry and caring, she recalls. Today she views her brothers as mentors, and both of them as high achievers.

Their father's first business was a deli named Cohen's on Fairfax in Los Angeles, which he bought with his brother Peter in 1940. They kept the name and the place until they sold it to Cantor's, and each went on their own. David opened a luncheonette at Eighth and Los Angeles

David and Bella Zide in front of the Roll N' Rye Restaurant and Delicatessen, 1981.

downtown, the original Roll N' Rye, and Peter opened his own place on Spring Street.

In this downtown milieu, Rita learned the business—and how to interact with people—as a small child. At seven, eight, and nine years old, she made lunch runs to offices, at a time when it was still safe for a little girl to walk alone on the downtown streets.

"It was a blast," she remembers. "Everyone thought it was real cute, having such a young delivery girl. And for me it was big time including the camaraderie with those secretaries in those big buildings and meeting their big-name bosses. Wow."

Rita also learned how to cashier in the luncheonette. "In fact, we all learned the business inside-out, from cutting meat to working behind that big round counter to meeting people. We were taught how to be good to our customers and our employees, and how to set an example by putting energy into our work."

In 1963 David recognized Culver City as a developing area, and took a

The entire Roll N' Rye staff awaiting the completion of Roll N' Rye's new home.

One of Rita's famous pre-school Roll N' Rye tours.

calculated risk. He moved his restaurant with its warm and friendly atmosphere into a community unfamiliar with a deli-style motif. In what was then the new Studio Village Shopping Center, David was assisted by his sons, Sol and Abe, and even by young Rita behind the counter. Bella served as hostess. Combining excellent food with fair pricing and personal service, the Zide's enterprise took off.

Rita remembers her father as one with charisma, a big-hearted, happy-go-lucky man who "instilled a great value system in his children. From my mother we learned self-esteem and hope for the future."

There were other influences in

Rita's early years. From age eight she played classical and blues piano; and in college (at San Jose State, where she majored in psychology and minored in history) she played guitar and sang, adding soft rock to her repertoire. For a time she thought she would be a teacher.

But the restaurant business was her first love, her first on-the-job training, and it fit very naturally into her adult life. In 1973 Rita bought the restaurant from her father, becoming sole proprietor. She maintained its essential elements—her parents' congeniality and food-preparation savvy—while adding her unbridled energy and contagious enthusiasm.

At about the same time, her brothers started their own successful restaurants that carry their names: "Solley's" in Woodland Hills and Sherman Oaks; and "Abe's" in Northridge.

"Now I could do all the things I wanted to do—not radical changes, you understand," she adds quickly. "It was always family oriented. Besides, I'm not into trends. But it was mine; mine to refurbish and mine to create a sense of family among staff."

That feeling of family also extends to some of her clientele, the "regulars" who have been coming here for 30 years. Waitresses often know customers by name. Some sit in the

same place, especially the early break-fasters who arrive when the restaurant opens at 6 a.m., and usually order the same thing.

"It's sort of like *Cheers* here—a place where everybody knows your name—and each other. Here is where they know they will get quality, quantity, and personal service. I just think people should enjoy life, leave their troubles outside and come in and have a good time."

Rita tells her employees that if people come in grumpy they can help them to turn their mood around. Make them so pleased with their food and service that they leave happy.

Employee Lee Caffrey takes it one step further: "The people who come in here do love the food, but they also like the sense of community. It's a real gathering place."

The Roll N' Rye is so busy it demands hard work from the staff; but Rita's philosophy of enjoying yourself is the core of staff training. Says Manager Simone Castron, a 13-year employee: "We believe you should be happy on the job, and our longtime employees prove it. Some have been here 20 years, because there is a really good feeling, working here. Rita is fun and open. She expects a lot, but gives a lot in return."

Several of the Roll N' Rye's support staff prove the point further with their seniority and outstanding reputations: Solomon Perez, known as the "King of the Matzo Balls," is approaching 20 years; Howard Kravitsky, one of the last good deli men, is an 18-year employee; and Eddie King, a 15-year employee, is a top-notch "left hand" in the back.

(Left to right) Simone Castron, 13-year Roll N' Rye manager; Rita Zide, owner, 30 years at Culver City location; and Howard Kravitsky, 18 years with Roll N' Rye, inside the construction shell of the new Roll N' Rye location.

At one time Rita even had three generations of one family working for her: the late Stella Woolston, her daughters Liz Carmen and Barbara Tarbox, and Barbara's daughter Suzie Bigelow, now her night manager. "My grandmother worked here 25 years, and my mother 12 years. I literally grew up here," Suzie recalls.

When the shopping center was re-developed, and the new Roll N' Rye opened in February 1990, it increased business volume by 30 percent. The staff had many new patrons to get to know.

Tearing down the old restaurant with its family memories was traumatic

Rita toasting the new Roll N' Rye construction with a "Dr. Brown's cream soda salute."

for Rita. With effort, she kept the old restaurant going during most of the construction and move-in to the new site just yards away, for continuity and her patrons' convenience.

"I don't believe in advertising because this business was built by word-of-mouth. But during the transition, I did run progress reports in the local paper to keep people informed."

During the actual move, when all the employees pitched in to make it as smooth as possible, there was a 10-day break between leaving the old and opening the new. To maintain a bond with her customers, Rita pitched a huge tent in the parking lot, put a heater in it, and served Continental breakfasts from her makeshift set-up. That lasted until the weather turned bad and high winds caused her to close down for five days.

Customers readily forgave the disruption, but some worried aloud that the new size and volume would change the atmosphere. Would the restaurant maintain its reputation for generous quantities of delicious food? Would the atmosphere be as homey?

The answer was yes on both counts. The design was kept comfortable—in light and airy ivory with hunter-green touches, the same historical photo blow-ups of Culver City's horse-and-buggy days lining the walls, and the same bevelled glass accents. Add to that the sight and scent of the food, with rows of hanging kosher salami; a deli-case filled with trays of olives, cream cheese, ham, roast beef, pickles, smoked herring, assorted knishes, and much more. On top of the deli counter sit baskets of fresh bagels and Kaiser and French rolls. Shelves behind the counter are stacked with loaves of pungent fresh rye and egg bread, boxes of matzos, and jars of gefilte fish.

Early reviews on the new Roll N'

Rye noted, "The walls may be new but it's the same great place," and "unassuming and comfortable, it's like a pat on the back from a good friend."

Indeed, the Grand Opening in February 1990 was a huge success. Customers of all ages jammed the new restaurant to give it their taste tests. Employees were on the run to keep up with the overflow crowd. And Rita, pleased as she was to see her plans fall into place, found it all very emotional. "I hadn't realized how much building the new restaurant, and following my father's example, really meant to me until then."

Rita is known for her high energy and spirited approach to life. "In our old place, I worked the line a lot (behind the counter)," she says. "It kept me in touch." In the new place she likes to table-hop frequently to say hello to old friends.

The restaurant does get attention in unlikely places—through its T-shirts and sweatshirts. Customers run into others wearing the shirts in faraway locales like New York and Japan.

The Roll N' Rye is also noted for its special events at home. On Halloween Rita gets the biggest pumpkin she can find, and has a "judge the weight" contest at a party for patrons' children and grandchildren. Then the cooks make fresh pumpkin pie for a special—and free—Thanksgiving dinner

Interior of the original Culver City Roll N' Rye.

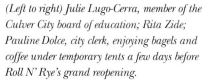

for senior citizens.

Now an annual event, the restaurant closes for an afternoon to host dinners for seniors from the Freda Mohr Multiservice Center in the Fairfax District who otherwise would be alone for the holiday. It is a happy, spiritual event of sharing memories, singing old songs, and giving a flower to each there.

During the Jewish holidays of Passover and Rosh Hashanah, the restaurant also serves seder dinners for those who like to congregate at the restaurant rather than stay at home.

The events are part of management's ongoing community involvement, which includes belonging to

(Left to right) Julie Lugo-Cerra, member of the Culver City board of education; Rita Zide; Pauline Dolce, city clerk, enjoying bagels and coffee under temporary tents a few days before Roll N' Rye's grand reopening.

numerous civic organizations and sponsoring group activities. One that especially "recharges my batteries," Rita says, "is conducting tours for schoolchildren on field trips. We show them little things, like how we make our own pickles. Their curiosity and enthusiam are heart-warming."

What's next, people often ask Rita Zide, now that the new restaurant is well established and has taken its larger volume in stride. "Who knows?" she answers. "Someday maybe a second restaurant. Every challenge I've had, I've met and enjoyed.

"I'd love to cut a record in a studio someday, just for the fun of it," she says, confessing her ongoing love of music. "I guess I've got a little Bette Midler in me."

But for now her dynamic business in the ever-growing local community will keep her busy for some time to come. New foods to offer. More people to meet. More customers to keep happy.

Century 21 – Dan Cavanaugh Realtors

Sixty-five years ago, the building that now houses Dan Cavanaugh's real estate business was something quite different. It was one of Culver City's earliest banks—the Culver City Commercial & Savings Bank. Cavanaugh can prove it by showing you the sturdy old vault with its thick protective walls, now pressed into service as a storage area.

"I bought the building in 1961 after it had been altered from 25 feet wide down to 15 feet to expand the street," explains Cavanaugh, who operates his present-day business with son Dan Jr. "Even though it was a small structure, it had a prime location [at 9352 Venice Boulevard] then as now."

Dan Sr. enjoys looking at the old deeds and tracing the former institution's history—which includes the fact that Cecil B. DeMille once served as its president.

There have been plenty of changes in the real estate business, too, Cavanaugh points out. "When I began, it was a matter of punching doorbells to get new business," he says. "At first I almost starved to death, but I managed to break in by going door to door and sending out penny postcards to advertise."

Cavanaugh got his broker's license in 1949, four years after he got out of the service and moved to California. An Ohioan by birth, he worked for the Gas

Company in the accounting department before he took the plunge into real estate. His "doorbell" and "penny postcard" days were spent with another company, and stretched into eight years before he moved on. Then, in 1961, when he bought the little bank building, he used only the front and rented out the back portion for $40 a month.

Cavanaugh's wife worked in the business with him in the beginning,

Reflecting the enormous growth in Culver City real estate value over the past 25 years or so, a 1965 sign at Dan Cavanaugh Realtors stands in sharp contrast to a recent sign at the same Culver City location. Culver City real estate investments have been, and will continue to be solid investments for home buyers.

before Dan Jr. grew up and joined him officially. She continues to do the bookkeeping from home. (The Cavanaughs also have a daughter, Shelley, who is involved in apartment ownership and management.)

"One thing in favor of the real estate business in the late forties," he recalls, "you couldn't find an apartment anywhere. But houses were springing up all over the place, even being sold furnished for under $12,000."

Today's business, under the banner "Century 21-Dan Cavanaugh Realtors," includes residential sales as well as commercial sales in retail and small office space and apartment building sales. Part of the Century 21 family since 1973, the Cavanaughs now have 25 salespersons.

"We believe Culver City has maintained its small-town atmosphere," Dan Jr. notes. "You can still get very involved here, and we do; you know so many people around town and you can feel like your participation makes a difference."

Their activities include serving on the chamber of commerce, planning commissions, the board of realtors, and school and church support groups.

"Often our clients represent several generations in one family," Dan Sr. says, adding, "They are also our long-time friends."

Didi Hirsch Community Mental Health Center

What happens when a depressed person threatens suicide, a drug-user hallucinates, an elderly man or woman quits eating, a child wants to die? For more than 50 years the Didi Hirsch Community Mental Health Center has been responding to these heartbreaking calls for help.

An established, comprehensive mental health agency that provides a full range of treatment and prevention services, the Didi Hirsch Center covers mental health needs not only in Culver City but other Southland communities as well.

The highly visible, extremely busy center at 4760 South Sepulveda Boulevard in Culver City offers crisis intervention; therapy for children, adults, and families; special services for the elderly, including community adult day-care; after-hours emergency help; outreach and educational programs; outpatient programs for drug-abuse treatment, and a number of other services.

The need for adult psychiatric service in the community came into focus after the 1929 stock market crash and subsequent Great Depression. A group of women banded together in 1931 to provide care for a sample group of unemployed. Their

The Didi Hirsch Community Mental Health Center facility at 4760 South Sepulveda Blvd. in Culver City opened in 1974.

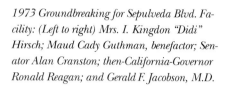

1973 Groundbreaking for Sepulveda Blvd. Facility: (Left to right) Mrs. I. Kingdon "Didi" Hirsch; Maud Cady Guthman, benefactor; Senator Alan Cranston; then-California-Governor Ronald Reagan; and Gerald F. Jacobson, M.D.

efforts were so impressive that eventually they grew to become Los Angeles Psychiatric Services (in 1942). Now the city had its first community-based adult outpatient psychiatric clinic.

Support today comes from both public and private sectors, with the United Way, the County of Los Angeles, United Hostesses' Charities, Culver City Guidance Clinic Guild, and the Los Angeles County Department of Health Services among the most prominent sponsors. Through the efforts of the center's namesake, the late Didi Hirsch, The United Hostesses' Charities and other philanthropic groups, major fund-raising was accomplished for the new building completed in 1974. At this time, too, the Culver City Guidance Clinic Guild joined with Didi Hirsch CMHC to inaugurate the center's Family and Child Guidance Clinic Division.

Under the guidance of the late Gerald F. Jacobson, M.D., executive

director for 28 years until his death in 1987, the center grew to serve over 9,000 clients each year, and reaches some 13,000 more through prevention and education programs.

"A hallmark of our successful history has been our effort to make mental health services available to as many persons as possible through the center and satellite locations," explains Ann Lodwig Brand, Ph.D., the current executive director.

Beyond Culver City, the center has residential services for special groups. Excelsior House in Inglewood is the newest satellite facility, offering intensive on-site treatment and rehabilitation. Jump Street is a short-term residential facility in Los Angeles for the homeless and mentally ill, and Harbor Gateway Clubhouse in Gardena is a socialization, case management, and outreach program. Via Avanta, based in Pacoima, is a dedicated substance abuse division that serves men, women, pregnant women, and women with children. And in the Venice Division there are two distinct programs, for drug treatment and for broad-based mental health counseling.

The center's mission is to give priority to those in greatest need regardless of the ability to pay. Serving a diversity in cultures and languages, the center's staff of 200 includes psychiatrists, psychologists, clinical social workers, and specialized counselors. They are aided by many dedicated volunteers.

The Didi Hirsch Center has played a leading role in Los Angeles and the nation, not only in developing mental health services and programs, but in establishing an extensive referral network with other agencies and provider groups.

The Culver Studios

Symbolic of The Culver Studios' illustrious past, its handsome white plantation mansion at 9336 West Washington Boulevard is the centerpiece of all present-day activity. Set behind a broad expanse of lawn and a graceful circular drive, the colonial structure fronts the lot where *Gone With The Wind* was filmed—and where Atlanta was burned.

The mansion—more than 70 years old and listed on the local historical register—has more than a pretty face, however. It houses administration offices for a very busy working lot that supports production for movies, television shows, commercials, and music videos.

Much history has been made here since the studio's opening in 1919. Its legacies include the pioneering vision of founder Thomas H. Ince, the grandiose sets of one-time owner Cecil B. DeMille, and the brilliant miniatures used in *King Kong*.

The studio has attracted some of Hollywood's most legendary figures and has figured in many of the industry's greatest achievements. Gloria Swanson, Fred Astaire, Ginger Rogers, Orson Welles, Alfred Hitchcock, Lassie, and Steven Spielberg, among others, have worked at The Culver Studios. Over the years it has been home not only to Ince and DeMille but RKO Pictures, David O. Selznick, Howard Hughes, Desilu, Grant Tinker, and GTG Entertainment.

Referring to the lot's rich history, which has been a breeding ground for greatness and scandals alike, studio president Jack Kindberg points to the many Oscars and Emmys spawned here, and notes, "Perhaps most significantly this has been a studio that reflects change." Bo Jackson, Michael J. Fox, and Michael Jackson have been as comfortable shooting commercials here as were Clark Gable and Vivien Leigh in creating their larger-than-life roles as Rhett Butler and Scarlett O'Hara.

The studio functions as a permanent production facility. According to Robert Sirchia, vice president, operations, "We rent stages and offices to producers who come in and build their own sets. We have a prop department, a scene dock with sets and walls, a lighting and grip department, a commissary, a dispensary with emergency medical services, screening and editing, and a telecommunications department—all the support facilities needed to do the work."

With Kindberg and Sirchia each having more than a dozen years at the studio, the two men have worked as a team to create a service-based organization striving for value in cost, location, and level of service.

Some 120 employees back them up, while about 500 to 600 others are on the lot at any given time to create an average of 50 productions per year. The studio's physical plant includes 14 sound stages, about one-third of which are used for television. Of course, in the early days it was all movie production.

Founder Thomas Ince, whose career was cut short by an untimely death at the age of 44, is known for his lasting contributions to the growth of the film industry. Ince founded the studio in 1919, and achieved most of his fame as a director. But it was really his ability to assert himself as both producer and administrator that led to his ultimate success.

A true pioneer, he introduced a meticulous system for running the studio, shooting films in strict adherence to the scripts, and creating a self-contained workplace on the grounds.

Ince built his first studio in Santa Monica, at what is now the juncture of Sunset Boulevard and the Pacific Coast Highway. He assembled an elaborate collection of sets and production facilities that were literally a global village, with Dutch, Japanese, Irish, East Indian, and American Indian sets. Here, at what was called Inceville, from 1911 to 1915 the Western genre really took form.

Ince got involved with other ventures that led him to Culver City, including the group that built the former MGM lot here. When he became an independent producer in 1919, he paid $35,000 for 14 acres on Washington Boulevard, and began building his own studio. In January 1919 the colonial mansion was completed, and Thomas H. Ince Productions moved in.

Glamour and glitz intrigued Ince, and he promoted both along with the industry. He was known as a master of self-promotion, practiced the art well, and his studio flourished because of it.

Upon Ince's death, his widow sold the studio to Cecil B. DeMille, known for his grandiose productions. In his four-year tenure at what became the DeMille Studios, he produced his all-time big budget picture, *The King of Kings*. The monumental temple of Jerusalem set he built towered over the lot for a dozen years before being torched as part of the burning of Atlanta for *Gone With The Wind*.

An unexpected influence in the person of Joseph P. Kennedy entered the picture in 1926. Kennedy persuaded Harvard University to view films as an important art form by packaging a lecture series of Hollywood greats. An instant hero with the movie moguls, Kennedy then became the force behind the RKO-DeMille-Pathe merger, and more prosperity and growth for the "lot behind the mansion."

This led to complete RKO control by 1928, with DeMille leaving on good terms, and David Sarnoff and Joseph Kennedy as active heads of operation. During RKO's tenure on the lot, Joe Kennedy had his famed love affair with leading lady Gloria Swanson. The couple never kept the affair secret, and Kennedy built Swanson her own cottage/dressing room on the lot. He spent a great deal of time in California until 1929, when he sold off his motion picture interests and returned to Wall Street.

1920: The Thomas Ince Studios, in its first fgull year of operation, surrounded by citrus groves and open fields

RKO-Pathe Studios merged officially the following year and controlled the lot for nearly 30 years, bringing stardom to Bette Davis, Robert Mitchum, Cary Grant, and Katharine Hepburn, among others. It was a prolific period, with three blockbuster names emerging in the 1930s: King Kong, Fred Astaire, and Ginger Rogers. Kong, with its pioneering use of special effects, became a timeless classic. Astaire and Rogers, with their dynamic dancing and flashy production numbers, proved wildly successful.

Still under RKO-Pathe ownership, a new era began when David O. Selznick, a former RKO executive producer, formed Selznick International Pictures and housed it here. His objec-

tive: To produce only pictures of the highest quality. With some early successes, and other learning experiences, Selznick put together a plan to release 12 pictures at a total cost of $9 million. For this he needed more space, so by 1936 he was leasing the entire lot. The Selznick Wing was added to the east end of the mansion that year, and more stages were built.

Selznick's work in this period began with *A Star is Born* and ran to *Tom Sawyer*, *Intermezzo*, and *Rebecca*. His most memorable, of course, was *Gone With The Wind* in 1939.

The year's Oscar winner, this production had a scope was greater than anything Hollywood had seen to date. One of the most astounding facts about the production is that 1,400 women were interviewed for the part of Scarlett O'Hara, and 90 took screen tests at a cost of more than $90,000. In one year the picture had been seen by 25 million people. It was Selznick's finest hour.

The decade between 1940 and 1950 was historical for the studios, but a period of turbulence for Selznick. He divorced Louis B. Mayer's daughter Irene and married longtime love Jennifer Jones, and his financial losses in certain ventures sent him into bankruptcy in early

1949. At that time he left the lot.

Elsewhere on the lot, Alfred Hitchock and Orson Welles were enjoyed great success in this period. In the case of *Citizen Kane*, the 1940 film was widely acclaimed as one man's single most important contribution to the art. Orson Welles received Academy Award nominations for best director, best actor, best picture, and best screenplay, the latter an honor he won with fellow writer Herman J. Mankiewicz.

The influence of Howard Hughes affected the studios in 1950, when the multimillionaire tycoon and movie producer acquired it following an RKO-Pathe reorganization. His reputation as ruthless and despotic drove talent away

in droves. He produced a few unsuccessful movies, then sold the property to the General Tire and Rubber company's owners, who in turn sold to Desilu Productions. The year was 1956, and television had come of age.

Danny Thomas Productions occupied space on the lot at one time. The back lot was home to the "Andy Griffith Show" and "Hogan's Heroes." Many of TV's early classics were done here, including "The Untouchables," and "Wyatt Earp."

When Paramount purchased the studio in 1967, shows like "Peyton

In 1933 the classic motion picture King Kong *was filmed at The Culver Studios, known at the time as RKO-Pathe Studios.*

Place" and "Batman" came to life. But the late 1960s and early 1970s were not lively times in Hollywood. The movie industry in Los Angeles was ailing, with too few productions for available stage space. Studios began selling off back lots to cut losses, and The Culver Studios was no exception.

In December 1977 Joseph R. Laird bought the property for its real estate value. As Laird International Studios, it remained dormant through July 1979, basically in disrepair. Business began to pick up in 1980, and continued to improve throughout the 1980s.

In a joint venture between Grant A. Tinker and the Gannett company, in 1988 the property became The Culver Studios and home base of GTG Enter-

tainment. GTG began an extensive makeover project at the studio, which retained the classic design of the Ince era, but added new sound stages, underground parking, and refurbished offices.

The Culver Studios became a part of the Sony Pictures Entertainment family in mid-1991, although it maintains its own identity as a rental facility.

As the eastern anchor of the soon-to-be-refurbished downtown area, the presence of The Culver Studios reinforces Culver City's motto, "The Heart of Screenland."

Recent features produced here, of which the studio's personnel are especially proud, include *The Natural* with Robert Redford; *ET*'s interior production; *Raging Bull* with Robert DeNiro;

1990: The Culver Studios, beginning its 70th year of operation. This photo was taken upon completion of a $25-million renovation effort.

Airplane with Leslie Nielson and Robert Stack; *Beetlejuice* with Michael Keaton; and a host of popular Steve Martin movies. And Columbia's *Bugsy* and *Hook* used The Culver Studios lot for a solid portion of filming.

Jin's Shell

Jin Kwak, who came to the United States with $100 to his name, stayed on to make his dreams come true. As a proud naturalized citizen he built a thriving business and with his wife raised four accomplished children who continue to live Kwak's—and the American—dream.

Such is the stuff of Jin Kwak's success. Born in Korea, he came to the United States on a student visa in August 1966. To help support himself in those early days, he worked in a restaurant as a busboy and dishwasher while he pursued pharmacy studies. To this day he recalls those humble beginnings every time he dines in that restaurant.

Kwak went to work in a pharmaceutical lab after his training, but became interested in a service station dealership in 1971 when a friend opened his own Shell station. Kwak followed suit, with his first dealership at Washington Place and Sawtelle. By his own admission, he knew nothing about cars. "I had to learn the hard way," he recalls.

Within the year, Kwak opted out. Discouraged, he sold his station and went back to the pharmaceutical lab. But one night as he slept, he experienced a vivid dream: "I saw myself carrying a million dollars in my arms to the bank. That very day Shell called to offer me another station, and I thought, 'Well, this is my chance.'" It was his present-day site

at 10332 Culver Boulevard.

Kwak decided to try again, so with the proceeds from the sale of his first station he became both a new business owner and home owner. From a Culver City councilman, he bought the house he and his family still live in today.

"We took a big chance, and it meant working from dawn until dusk," Kwak notes. "Before long we found ourselves in the middle of a gasoline crisis (in 1973), so from that standpoint my decision to get back in was well-timed."

Now the Culver City station has more than eight employees and is one of eight stations in the Kwak chain stretching from Ventura to Anaheim.

In his dawn-to-dusk days, Kwak became a licensed mechanic, and went through Shell's extensive training program to provide professional service

in tune-up, air conditioning, wheel alignment, brakes, and smog licensing. For its emphasis on service, Jin's Shell has won awards from the local police force, the chamber of commerce, and Shell Oil Company itself as a valued dealership.

Kwak and his wife Young Hee had married in 1967, after she experienced an immigration snafu that forced her to come to California by way of El Salvador and Florida from Korea. Young Hee assisted Jin in the business from the start and currently is taking further Shell training.

The Kwak's four children, who also have worked in the business, take after their ambitious parents. All four are products of the Culver City school system. Karen, the oldest, is about to graduate from USC; Kenneth, next in line, is at West Los Angeles City College; Carolyn attends San Diego State; and Kevin is a senior and football player at Culver City High School.

Through his family's influence and support, Kwak became deeply involved with civic activities: as a member of the YMCA's Golden Circle; member of the board of education; on the Sister-City Committee that works with communities in Japan, Canada, Mexico, and Korea. "We've invested all of our adult lives here," Kwak says, "and we feel we want to give something back to the community that has been so good to us."

Center Paint & Wallpaper

Jordan Smith, Center Paint & Wallpaper's owner since early 1989, really believes " . . . the more things change, the more they stay the same." True, Culver City has grown tremendously since the business was founded in 1948. And products have changed to meet complex environmental demands. But Center Paint & Wallpaper's focus on customer service and hard work have remained constant.

"With that philosophy, we don't think our customers even realized we changed management," Smith says of his purchase from Sam Paperny, founder and former owner.

Paperny officially opened shop at a nearby location after he mustered out of the service. He quickly saw an opportunity for expansion by moving to the new "shopping center" at 11170 West Washington Boulevard, just across the street from Center Paint's present address (11153). The *Culver-Palms Post* described the shopping center's introduction as the "spectacular opening of the Washington-Sepulveda building, the newest ultra-modern structure" in the city. One block long, it housed seven shops. Among Paperny's neighbors: a physician-surgeon, a laundromat, and the Auto Club.

From the start, Paperny called his business Center Paint & Wallpaper. And from the beginning, he dealt in paints, varnishes, lacquers, and wallpaper.

"In that post-World War II economy, everything was growing," Paperny recalls. "I was young and my needs were very little. I was willing to work hard, so the business grew fast, with the city."

The advent of the GI home—which then cost about $10,500 with $500 down—meant people bought more often than they rented. In fact, rentals were hard to find, as tract homes were built by the thousands. The "do it yourself" era was born, and Center Paint helped provide the supplies, though scarce after the war.

In the "good old days" with less traffic and no parking problems, there were other challenges to face: Before flood control was put in, Paperny and his staff had to sandbag the property for protection. Once, his deliveryman got stuck in floodwaters at the corner of Culver and Center, and Paperny's new 1949 Plymouth was ruined. It needed new upholstery and a new motor.

Four years later Paperny built Center Paint's current building (4,000 square feet now next door) and added on 5,400 square feet in 1965. He remains active in property management.

Jordan Smith came to Culver City in 1953 from Boston, and gravitated to Paperny's shop because his grandfather and uncle back home were in the business. Still in school when he helped his uncle drive out to California, Smith admits, "I fell in love with California then, but I had to go home long enough to finish school and marry my Boston sweetheart." In 1957 the Smiths moved to California for good. Smith continued to work with Paperny, and now Smith's son is involved in the business, too.

Center Paint & Wallpaper's clientele includes individuals and companies, small and large accounts, homeowners, contractors, and industrial customers interested in specialty products.

"We believe there is a trend in the country toward basic service," Smith points out. "Even the large chain stores are finding that out. For us, the so-called new values of service and product knowledge are ones that we've employed all along."

Center Paint & Wallpaper has been serving the Culver City community since 1948. Its current location is 11153 Washington Boulevard.

Southern California Nursery, Inc.

When the Shinmotos describe their Southern California Nursery as a family business, they aren't kidding. For more than 40 years, the nursery has provided a livelihood for the offspring of Tsunetaro and Haruyo Shinmoto—namely Tony, the late Herky, Min, and Mitsy—and their families.

About half the staff of 16 are family members at the nursery's 5526 South Sepulveda Boulevard location and nearby growing yard. If the Shinmotos have longevity in their business, so do many of their customers, who have been buying their indoor and outdoor plants, supplies, and accessories for three generations.

The Shinmoto family history in America dates back to 1923, when Tsuneo Anthony (Tony), then five months old, and his parents landed in San Francisco from Hiroshima, Japan. The family moved south—first to Upland, California, where Kiyoto (Herky) and Minoru (Min) were born, then to Kingsburg, a small farming community about 20 miles south of Fresno, where Mitsuko (Mitsy) was born.

Around 1930 the family moved to Los Angeles and grew up in the Normandie-Exposition area, attending local grammar and junior high schools. In the summer of 1939 the Shinmotos moved back to Kingsburg and remained there until World War II.

The war interrupted any attempt at normalcy in the Shinmotos' lives. Forcibly evacuated by the U.S. government from their home, the family was moved to an internment camp at Gila River, Arizona. Tony had already graduated form Kingsburg High, but Herky and Min finished high school in camp. Mitsy later graduated from Venice High after the war.

Tony says his world was "pretty

Seated, left to right: Tsunearo, Mitsy, and Haruyo Shinmoto. Standing, left to right: Min, Herky, and Tony Shinmoto.

small then, but I remember the difficult camp life and the loss of our beloved used Chevy." The family, along with thousands of others, also lost their constitutional rights as American citizens and legal residents.

Herky and Min were drafted from the internment camp and served in the U.S. Army as linguists and interpreters during the occupation of postwar Japan. All Asians were ineligible for naturalization rights at that time, so Tony was classified as an "enemy alien" and thus not subject to draft as were his younger brothers. During the war, Tony took his parents and sister to Nebraska and Iowa to work in hotels and on farms to eke out a living.

In late 1945 the family returned to Southern California, and Tony and his father started to work in the gardening service area. When Herky and Min returned from military service, the family decided to do something more substantial. They started the nursery that ultimately would support four families, opening their doors in March 1948.

"My mother just shook her head and said it wouldn't work," Tony recalls with a smile. "She kept saying,

'You boys are too honest,' believing we'd give our profits away."

In the beginning the Shinmotos had very little capital, few customers, and great enthusiasm. The brothers used to wrangle over who would get to serve those who did come in. They also continued gardening services in the early years to ensure cash flow, and did landscape contracting for more than 20 years (from about 1950 to 1970) during the area's major development.

For the first seven years the family worked seven days a week to get established. Some fellow nurserymen had an ongoing wager as to when the Shinmoto's nursery would go out of business, especially when Sepulveda Boulevard underwent a major (half a street closure at a time) improvement, two years after the nursery opened. Marriages and children also brought about changes, along with a redistribution of duties.

Tony relinquished his position as corporate president in July 1991, but is still in charge of administrative matters. His wife Betty took over as president and is active in many phases of the business. They have three children: Julie, a pharmacist; Lynn, an attorney; and Mark, also a pharmacist.

Left to right: Yoko, Betty, Tony, Dorothy, and Min Shinmoto.

Minoru "Min" Shinmoto served in Japan as an interpreter and interviewer of civilians returning from Manchuria after the end of World War II.

When Herky died suddenly on August 8, 1981, his wife Yoko took his position as treasurer and is an active business partner. Their only daughter Kathy is a registered nurse.

Min gave up his post as corporate secretary in July 1991 but remains as general manager. His wife Dorothy is active in the business and is the present secretary. Their daughter Tracy Ann works in personnel at El Camino College. Their son Steve (a former co-manager of Southern California Nursery) and his brother Craig started their own business, a wholesale plant/tree nursery in partnership with Paul Nishikubo (also a former co-

manager of Southern California Nursery) in May 1991.

Sister Mitsy Matsuo, now a widow, is a landscape consultant and designer. She worked during the start of the business before she married and has recently returned to oversee the growing yard.

The brothers blended very different work styles and business philosophies in creating their business. Tony, a go-getter by nature, was determined to make sure the business would "put food on the table and give our children opportunities my generation didn't have." Herky was more conservative and not as eager to take risks. Min struck a balance between his two brothers.

The Shinmotos chose Culver City for their business because of its wide-open opportunities. Their Sepulveda Boulevard location used to overlook the famous Venice celery fields, long since developed. They got good advice early on from an old time nurseryman who told them to purchase (not lease) the land on which their business would grow. So they pooled their meager resources to make what would be an outstanding investment, even though most investments in those postwar years were uncertain.

Southern California Nursery built

Herky Shinmoto's memorial garden was dedicated on November 14, 1989.

Kiyoto "Herky" Shinmoto served in an MP unit in postwar Japan as an interpreter.

its business on quality and services, working closely with customers. Their motto is: "A knowledgeable gardener is a happy customer." The staff, which has grown to include a young and ambitious team, take the time to talk to customers to ensure growing and plant maintenance success, ultimately creating return business.

Conscious of its role in the community, the nursery recently created and developed the Culver City Freeway Garden, dedicated in late 1989. Established as a memorial to brother Herky, the project on the northeast corner of Sepulveda and Centinela also marked the nursery's 40 years in business.

The beautification project involved the joint efforts of Caltrans, Los Angeles County, Culver City, the Sepulveda-Slauson Businessmen's Association, fellow nurserymen, vendors, and countless friends. Plans are being discussed with the above agencies to expand and improve the sloping background of the garden.

Says Tony, speaking for the Shinmoto family: "The garden also gave us an opportunity to express our gratitude to the community that has supported us and has been our home for so long."

Bun's Radiator Sales & Service

A memorable name . . . that's what the owners had in mind when they called their business Bun's Radiator Sales & Service. It had been known at first as Prettyman's Garage, after Asa Prettyman, who established the shop in 1920. But when it reopened after World War II, the shop took its name from one of the new staff members, "a fellow by the name of Bunnell," recalls today's president and major stockholder George Prettyman. "We borrowed his nickname because it was catchy, and it stuck."

Where it all began, circa 1920.

Bun's reopened not only with a new name but new specialties at the time—in carburetion, auto electricity, and radiator rebuilding. It continued to maintain the fine reputation of the business and of the family behind it; Asa had become an auto machinist and mechanic in the earliest days of the "horseless carriage," honing his trade and introducing applications ahead of their time.

The Prettyman family, in the Culver City area for most of the century, arrived in this country in the late sixteenth century to help settle Delaware; then in 1847 moved west on the Oregon Trail. In modern times the family moved progressively south, from Lewiston, Idaho, (Asa's birthplace) to San Francisco to Los Angeles.

"My mother's side, named Tomaseck, came to Los Angeles from Vienna and Bavaria," Prettyman relates. "My mother remembered going by horse and buggy to the Marina del Rey area to camp out on weekends. Only a few families lived at the beach then."

In 1910 Asa Prettyman pioneered auto mechanics: He would ride on the fenders of race cars on the local speedway to keep the motors tuned up. His abiding interest in cars then took him and his young wife to Sacramento for a time (George was born there), where Asa was superintendent of an early Ford agency. In time, he moved back to Los Angeles to open his shop.

Although George was raised in the shop at Florence and Vermont, he decided to join the Los Angeles Police Department in 1941. He had been inspired as a boy in the 1920s when he rode on Culver City Chief of Police Jimmy Cain's motorcycle. He had a 21-year career there as an officer and night-school police science instructor (with three years out as a Machinist's Mate First Class in the Coast Guard).

By 1959 Prettyman was working days in the shop and graveyard shift as a supervising sergeant. When he left the force in 1962, he put all his energies into the shop—specializing in heat-exchange services; moving the shop in 1966 to its current location at 11407 West Washington Boulevard; starting over as a one-man shop, then growing again to a staff of 18. He's constantly installing new technology, including an advanced water recycling system well ahead of others in the industry. In fact, until 1974 he manufactured his own radiator core.

George's son Lee mustered out of the army in 1966 and joined the firm. In 1976 he took over the shop and George phased out to a semi-retirement and some teaching around the country for the National Radiator Association. Now Lee, an expert in air-conditioning, runs the company's shop, Reno Radiator, in Nevada; longtime employee Lois Danzig became Culver City manager; and George continues his part-time status. But he's taken on still another career: He manages a 16-boat marina and adjacent luxury apartment complex while he enjoys his own diesel trawler.

And he still shares with the staff his father's wisdom through his own penchant for teaching: "From the first time I ever held a wrench, my father insisted I analyze everything completely, then include customers in the diagnosis. That way, they understand what is needed—and they'll keep coming back."

The Coombs Family

When members of the Coombs family reminisce about "the good old days" in Culver City, they have a lot to talk about: three generations of leadership in civic and business endeavors.

Today Ronald E. (Ron) Coombs carries on the tradition through his Washington Boulevard law firm Coombs & Coombs, Inc., a partnership formed with his father Ronald H. (Brick) Coombs, now retired.

The two men are descendants of Culver City pioneer Dan F. Coombs, Ron's grandfather, who was the first acting mayor, chairman of the board of trustees that governed before incorporation, the second mayor after cityhood, and a member of the city council for 13 years. Dan's wife Fleda was the first president of the Culver City PTA in 1917, and his brother Bill became chief of police.

A native of Vermont, Dan Coombs moved first to Alhambra, then Culver City, because of "all the open land." He established a building contracting business and built a number of well-known local landmarks, including City Hall and many houses.

Brick, so called for his red hair, and his younger brother Charles (Chick) were preschoolers when the family moved here. The brothers remember "weenie bakes" at the nearby creek, where they also learned to swim.

In the late 1930s, Brick—often mistaken for Red Skelton—went to Los Angeles College of Law, and in February 1939 was admitted to practice in the courts. Chick later became a noted author, writing more than 70 books on topics as diverse as aerospace and chil-

Ronald E. "Ron" Coombs (left) and Ronald H. "Brick" Coombs.

dren's subjects.

When Brick started his law practice, he shared space with the only other attorney in town. Then in the mid-1940s he opened an office in the historic Meralta Theater complex and became fast friends with the late Mayo D. Wright, a well-known insurance man.

"I remember that old theater well," says Ron, who was born in 1941. "I loved going to my dad's office there as a kid."

These were eventful years for Brick, too. In 1947 he survived a small-plane crash that killed one of Culver City's noted doctors en route to a fishing trip in Mexico. Brick was rescued a

harrowing three days later, with broken arms and legs.

He recovered and built a prominent law practice. With Mayo in 1953, he bought his law firm's current building, a distinctive ranch-style house converted to office space. (Some years later they added a front wing.) Then in the late 1950s Brick formed a partnership with attorney Horace Comstock. It lasted until 1972, at which time Ron became a partner and Comstock founded another firm in the same building. Ron joined in 1969 after earning a law degree from California Western University in San Diego.

Even then, Ron recalls, there weren't more than a dozen attorneys in Culver City. Now there are well over 100.

Coombs & Coombs, Inc., continues to specialize in probate and estate planning. Along with longtime secretary-paralegal staffers Yvonne Kalfsbeck, who had been with the firm since 1968, up to her untimely death in August 1991, and Georgina Knight, who joined in 1974, Coombs & Coombs continues to serve many clients who worked with Brick years ago.

Ron, whose teenage daughter Heather is still too young to declare an interest in the law, takes civic involvement as seriously as his father and grandfather did before him. He served for three years as chairman of the board of the Culver/Palms YMCA and as president of the Rotary Club and local bar association. "Civic involvement is key to our business philosophy," he notes, "to serve both personal and professional needs."

Culver City Animal Hospital

Personalized family practice for small animals—that was the common vision of two veterinarians, who, though born, raised, and educated 20 years apart, got together during their careers to make the Culver City Animal Hospital what it is today.

The practice, established by Joseph H. Adams, D.V.M., and later joined by Larry C. Kidwell, D.V.M., at 5830 West Washington Boulevard, has grown to serve three generations of Culver City-area families and their pets: mostly dogs and cats, some guinea pigs and rats, the occasional raccoon or snake, and, once, an elephant with a toothache.

Culver City Animal Hospital was begun in Cleveland, Ohio, in 1946 when Adams became an associate at a leading animal hospital there. He worked with a noted clinician and surgeon in the region, learning the ropes and formulating a strategy for building his own practice one day.

Adams, an Ohio State University graduate, class of 1938, had spent eight years with a federal government bureau for animals, working all around the U.S. before entering private practice in his native Ohio. By 1949, however, he was having repeated allergic outbreaks and was advised to try a warmer climate.

"I went out to California and within two weeks was all cleared up," Adams recalls. "I was encouraged by fellow veterinarians to take the California state board examinations, and put down roots. Quite a change for an Ohio boy. But I felt so much better, I thought, 'Why not?'"

In a hurry-up effort to meet the deadline, he quickly applied, borrowed textbooks for a quick review, and took the boards in 1950 "with a degree of apprehension. It was about 12 years after I'd completed

my schooling."

Adams went back to Ohio to await the results. Three months later he learned he had passed, sent in his license fees, and prepared to move his family to California. But a former colleague needed help keeping his practice afloat during an illness, so the Adams family delayed moving for 18 months.

"It sure wasn't easy to wait when my wife Pauline and our sons Howard and Dennis went out in midwinter of 1951 to take a look at California," Adams remembers. "There I

was in an Ohio blizzard, fighting snow just to get home from the office, and there they were, sending me pictures in shirtsleeves and shorts. That clinched it."

They moved West the following summer and Adams found work at once in his field. Within a year, he began looking for a suitable location for his own animal hospital. Of five possible locations, he chose the present site not only for its lot size and off-street parking capability but because he liked what he saw around town: "Well-maintained homes and

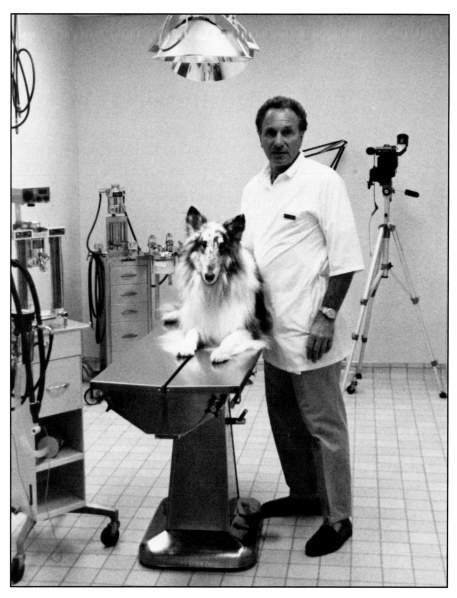

Dr. Larry Kidwell, shown here with a satisfied patient in the hospital's state-of-the-art surgical suite, joined the practice as a partner in 1965.

ABOVE: Culvr City Animal Hospital has earned a reputation for providing personalized, quality care.

LEFT: The spacious waiting room at Culver City Animal Hospital.

businesses. Friendly people. Good business opportunities."

Within a year the Culver City Animal Hospital was built, and it officially opened in March 1954. Its early staff: Adams and his wife Pauline. The practice grew quickly, however. Within three months he was able to hire assistants and give his wife "some free time to care for our sons." Growth was further enhanced when the Santa Monica and San Diego freeways were built nearby, making the business even more accessible.

Enter Dr. Kidwell, who walked into the hospital one day in 1964 and asked Adams if it was for sale. Adams gave a hearty "no" at the time, but had several subsequent meetings with Kidwell in which they discussed their goals and shared their professional plans. The two men's personalities meshed so well that they formed a partnership in January 1965.

"I met Dr. Adams through my employer at the time [Dr. Ben Klein, an-other Ohio State graduate] and was drawn to him because of his reputation," Kidwell explains. "He was known not only for his skill but for the ethical and conscientious way he worked."

Kidwell, a San Francisco native who graduated from the University of California, Davis, in 1958, brought to the partnership a high level of enthusiasm for developing the practice, and an outgoing personality polished by years in show business. "My father was a musician, and I worked my way through college as a trumpet player," he explains.

After graduation, Kidwell first went into the service as a captain in the Army Veterinary Corps before taking the job with Klein in 1961, then partnering with Adams in 1965.

Soon they remodeled and expanded, doubling the practice and creating an exceptional facility at a time when modern animal hospitals were in their infancy. Based on models of UCLA and Cedars-Sinai, the hospital is equipped with private surgeries, sophisticated X-ray and diagnostic equipment, an isolation ward, efficient examining rooms, comfortable "living quarters" for the small patients, and an enlarged night-attendant quarters. The bright, gleaming rooms and hallways are immaculate.

At about the same time, Kidwell expanded his family, marrying in 1966 and having sons Brent (now a journalism student at UC Irvine) in 1969 and Damon (an art student at Cal Arts in Valencia) in 1971.

Over the years the partners have treated many pets with famous owners from the studios. Adams recalls Charles Bickford as "a gentle giant of a man who once stood [here] with tears streaming down his face, hand-feeding his sick pet." Yul Bryner had a black German shepherd, a black cadillac with black interior and always wore black leather clothes.

And there have been regulars—Rod Stewart with his collies, John Candy with his menagerie of dogs and cats. Elvis Presley and then-wife Priscilla brought their Great Danes Snoopy and Brutus to Kidwell. Elvis was a softie when it came to pets—he had a chow with a congenital kidney condition. Rather than restricting the dog's movement, he allowed it to roam around Graceland with a weak and uncontrollable bladder. Then there was Sammy Davis Jr. When asked why he had a Great Dane that he was afraid of, he replied "Because it's cool, man."

Adams and his wife retired in 1977 to Arizona, where they could spend more time with their two grandchildren. Pauline Adams passed away in 1990 and Dr. Adams died in 1991.

Kidwell, an avid golfer who manages to get away with wife Sydney to the desert occasionally, continues his busy hands-on practice, treating 25 to 30 patients a day. With his support staff of 10, some with 18, 20, even 30 years' tenure, he perpetuates the family feeling indigenous to a community like Culver City.

Culver Park Realty – Dan Patacchia

His title is Mayor Emeritus for Life, though he needs no introduction to Culver City residents. His office at Culver Park Realty holds further proof of that, the walls lined with commendations that recognize more than 40 years of civic service.

Dan Patacchia's long and satisfying business career actually began with a restaurant back home in Pennsylvania. He had, however, been out to visit his brother, who drove limousines for the studios in Culver City, and he was smitten with the area. Five years later, in 1941, Patacchia and his wife Lillian made the move, and Patacchia also became a limousine driver, first with Pacific Nevada and then MGM, driving Gregory Peck (a particular favorite), Shirley Temple, Jennifer Jones, Elizabeth Taylor, and other big stars.

He got interested in real estate when he sold a vacant lot he'd purchased as an investment. In 1948 he received his broker's license and in 1950 opened an office, from which he dealt mostly with residential but some commercial properties.

Patacchia's staff has been as large as 20, though now he has scaled back to four, still operating from the office that he built in 1950 at 4240 Overland Avenue.

"I think the most satisfying part of my work has been helping people of modest means buy their first homes,"

he says. "One property I've sold eight different times, and each time the seller made a profit."

He became president of the Culver City Board of Realtors in 1956 and was elected regional vice president of the California Real Estate Association in 1959. His professional dedication has earned him the "Realtor of the Year" award three times from his peers.

Known as a gentleman in the truest sense of the word, Patacchia took a pragmatic approach to leadership. Even before he ran for public office, he helped deal with growth, serving as a mediator when 300 homes had to make way for freeways.

In 1960 he was elected to the city council, and he served an unprecedented six-year term as mayor from 1962 through 1968. When he ran for his second term, he received the highest vote total ever recorded for that office in Culver City. A registered Democrat running for a nonpartisan office, he was even endorsed by the Republican Club—a first at the time.

Patacchia's accomplishments belie his style—softspoken, patient, unassuming. His emphasis on efficient government won him a resolution from the state of California noting reduced taxes each year by incurring one of the lowest periods of bonded indebtedness in the entire state. His eye for redevelopment while in office helped annex and rezone what is now the Fox Hills Mall, and get a new police station built—one noted for its design and practicality, without a bond issue.

Patacchia stepped aside after his

second council turn due to a heart attack and subsequent surgery. But he has continued as an active volunteer and real estate professional since then. A member of the chamber of commerce since 1952, he resumed a directorship after his mayoral years and became president in 1971. In 1972 he was apppointed a member of the Marina Del Rey Small Craft Harbor Commission and in 1973 to the L.A. County Tax Assessment Appeals Board.

Patacchia's contributions have been enormous, but as a modest man he often seems as surprised as he is pleased by the accolades: Adult Citizen of the Year in 1989 by the Lions' Club; recipient of the Book of Golden Deeds from the Culver City Exchange Club, past president of the Exchange Club; charter member honors from Elks Lodge #1917; the chamber's Man of the Year; the Sister City Committee's representative to Japan and Mexico; and many more. Additionally, he serves as a director of Culver National Bank.

Patacchia and his wife have one daughter, two grandsons, and a great-grandson, Jimmy Dean Ericsson—the center of the Mayor Emeritus' attention these days.

Rolling Greens

"We started selling our plants from an old Chevy van," says Windy Overbach, president of Rolling Greens Nursery, Inc. "So you can see our name was a natural."

Windy, nicknamed as an infant by an uncle who refused to call him by his given name Irwin, gives his wife Yolanda credit for naming the business. He also calls her " . . . the magnet that draws designers and decorators" to their wholesale indoor plant salesroom because of her eclectic good taste in the accessories department that she manages.

Rolling Greens offers an array of accessories, from expensive Chinese bowls to clay and plastic pots to custom baskets. The mainstay of its business, however, is specimen interior plants and blooming plants (but no cut flowers). Sales are prominent in bromeliads, mums, cyclamen, Easter lilies, and poinsettias.

The inviting showroom is tucked away on a hillside officially addressed as 9528 Jefferson Boulevard, but actually located on Culver City's highest hill adjacent to the boulevard. The showroom is supported by a vast display area, which is attached, and warehouses terraced into the descending hillside.

With 21 employees now, about five persons are assigned solely to keeping the plant inventory cleaned up. Presentation is extremely important to Rolling Greens' business mode, which

Yolanda and Windy Overbach.

is a demanding look at the product and better acclimated plants that will live easily in buyers' environments.

The business has experienced solid growth every year since 1973, when Rolling Greens' goods were first dispensed from ill-fitting shelves in the van ("I built them myself, and they never worked right," Windy Overbach says with a laugh). The next step up was borrowing garages and carports—empty during the day when people were at work—for plant storage while the sales were being made.

From carports to a rented 1,200-square-foot greenhouse, Rolling Greens took two years to support buying one lot at its present location. By 1977 it supported a second greenhouse and two lots down the street, and in 1984 Rolling Greens acquired the middle piece for a continuous string of hillside property.

Overbach got interested in plants after he graduated from Cal State Hayward, where he met his wife. With a minor in business, he went to work

managing a cousin's plant shop on Melrose. From that vantage point, he saw a real need for a wholesale outlet.

"At first we sold only to plant shops, the carriage trade," he explains. "Now most of our sales are to decorators and designers, and more recently, hotels, amusement parks, and increasingly more corporate buyers."

Rolling Greens also offers short-term rentals for special events like weddings and bar mitzvahs. The company often donates plants and plant material to local groups for handicapped training or to brighten shelters for homeless women. On site, tours for schoolchildren are frequent and are fun for all.

And in the community, Rolling Greens regularly sponsors local festivals and other special events.

Their logo today portrays just what the Overbachs want their business personality to be: It's a pleasant little guy on roller skates—a personified potted plant—warm, friendly, and growing.

Brotman Medical Center

For more than 60 years, Culver City and West Los Angeles area residents have had access to primary healthcare services right in their own backyard. The Brotman Medical Center, with its campus that stretches from Delmas Terrace to Hughes to Washington and Venice boulevards, has grown with the community it serves to offer the foremost medical programs and technology available.

Today's Medical Center, with 495 beds and more than 1,000 employees, is large enough to provide a range of high technology services (advanced diagnostic expertise, Magnetic Resonance Imaging, CT Scan, and Linear Accelerator for radiology oncology). Yet the center is small enough to offer a high-touch response to patients' needs. It is also a highly active paramedic base station and part of the area's Emergency Medical Support network.

The center's progressive programs have roots that reach back to July 1927, when the facility—then known as the Heart of Screenland Hospital—was established. Its founder Wyant La Mont, M.D., and his mother Mary C. La Mont, R.N., opened an eight-bed obstetrics hospital at 3828 Hughes. It was chartered the follow-

Today's Brotman Medical Center, with 495 beds and more than 1,000 employees, offers the foremost medical programs and technology available.

Brotman Medical Center was called Culver City Hospital from 1941 to 1958.

ing July and its name was changed to University Hospital.

By 1935 there were 50 beds, 18 bassinets, an active medical staff of 18, and 8 graduate nurses. Rates were an incredible $6 to $10 per day for a private room.

In 1941 the facility officially became the Culver City Hospital, owned by A.E. Hoppe. The hospital staff grew to 64 by 1947, and the facility drew increasing recognition as a member of the American and California hospital associations, and Blue Cross.

Hoppe sold the hospital in 1958 to David M. Brotman, M.D., hence the David M. Brotman Memorial Hospital, and subsequent Brotman Medical Center, came to be. Under Dr. Brotman's tenure, which lasted until his death in 1973, the two landmark midrise buildings were constructed—one in 1962 and the other in 1970.

"In the 1980s the Medical Center grew into tertiary—or specialty—care for very ill patients," explains chief executive officer Ronald C. Phelps "That could only have happened with a combination of dedicated physicians and a high technology base."

The Hospital Corporation of America began a six-year ownership in 1981, then sold the facility to HealthTrust, Inc., a spinoff of 100 hospitals of which Brotman was the largest.

In June 1989 Brotman Partners LP, a joint venture between approximately 94 physicians and Republic Health Corporation, became the limited partnership that propels the Medical Center forward today. Through an innovative organizational plan the partners encourage cooperation and harmony between medical and administrative staff for greater excellence.

Exemplary of this interaction is the center's outstanding reputation in pathology, radiology, open heart surgery, and intensive care specialties. Significant new services include behavioral, psychology, and chemical dependency programs with inpatient, outpatient, day care, and residential living available.

Progressive plans for the 1990s focus on a new healthcare facility for women. In response to changing trends in birthing, there is a family oriented program with labor, delivery, recovery and post-partum care in one room; a pacesetting neonatal intensive care unit for sick babies; mammography; outreach education; counseling; and an extensive resource library.

E.V. Roberts & Associates

The numbers are impressive: 5,000 products in stock representing 15 leading manufacturers; up to 8,000 customers; and a 22,000-square-foot warehouse and custom-manufacturing facility.

The numbers represent the success of E.V. Roberts & Associates, Inc., a sales, service, and technical support business with a 50-plus-year history of providing chemicals, plastics, and adhesives for the aerospace, electronic, industrial, and transportation industries.

Almost 30 years of that history has been spent in Culver City. The company outgrew two locations before buying its current property at 8500 Steller in 1977.

"I had a soft spot for the area," explains president Ernest V. Roberts. "My family moved to Culver City from Canada in 1923 and I went through grammar and high school here, so it was like coming back to old friends."

He didn't have to move the business far—from several Los Angeles locations—although his own travels had taken him halfway around the world in the interim.

Before he and Leon Fry formed Fry & Roberts manufacturers' representatives in 1938, Roberts followed other interests: first theater management (from usher at the old Meralta Theater to manager), then radio operator (he was a commercial radio operator on seagoing vessels in the late 1920s). In the early 1930s he worked as a broadcast engineer and went to Southwestern University at night for his L.L.B.

"I never practiced law, but I kept up my interest in radio technology," he explains. As a civilian radio operator he flew on Royal Air Force military aircraft in 1940 to Singapore and Scotland, even though he had become a U.S. citizen and later served in the U.S. Marine Corps.

By 1945 Roberts was ready to buy out Fry's part of their business and concentrate on selling electronic parts and

components. He branched out in 1952 to become a distributor for chemicals and plastics, which ultimately became E.V. Roberts and Associates' primary business. (A personal note from 1953: Ernest married his secretary Madeleine, a native of France who has become an award-winning artist.)

The company does some customizing on site. As distributor for such well-known companies as 3M, Shell, General Electric, Loctite, and others, it buys basic raw materials in drums, then either adds materials or repackages as needed. Chemists on staff develop new formulations for customers, meeting

government specifications or designing a product for specific needs. Quality assurance and documentation are integral parts of the operation.

The firm has grown from one to 60 employees, with headquarters in Culver City, a sales office and warehouse in Hayward in Northern California, and sales offices in Denver and Seattle.

"There is great satisfaction in having a bootstrap operation grow to work with companies of international stature," Roberts notes, and as a civic booster and former Lions' Club president, "great personal pleasure of feeling so at home in the community."

Fox Hills Mall

At its inception the Fox Hills Mall was called the $70-million mall. Today the regional shopping center, created in 1975 by The Hahn Company, continues to be a major performer, consistently finishing among the top 10 producers for Hahn in gross sales. In 1990 Fox Hills had a mall-wide increase in sales of 8 percent, and generated $153 million in revenue for the year.

The mall, which provides thousands of Culver City jobs, serves the highly-competitive West Los Angeles trading area. With close to one million people, West Los Angeles is one of the nation's largest retail markets.

Built in Fox Hills, once home to a country club, the Red Riding Stable (in the 1930s and 1940s), and later a go-cart track, the mall was developed by The Hahn Company. The San Diego-based company, then known as Ernest W. Hahn, Inc., is the largest shopping center developer in the western United States, and the fourth-largest in the nation.

Hahn not only developed, but owns and manages the Fox Hills Mall as part of its 50-center, 35-million-square-foot property portfolio.

The mall is on the southeast corner of Slauson Avenue and Sepulveda Boulevard, easily accessible from nearby freeways and with plentiful parking. With nearly one million square feet of retail shops on three levels, the enclosed shopping center covers 50 acres. The mall opened 95 percent leased, with three major department stores—The Broadway, May Company, and JC Penney—plus fashion boutiques, gift and accessory shops, and restaurants.

Fox Hills Mall was the first of its kind in the Westside area, and it opened to great acclaim. Its rounded, "wavelike" paneled ceiling interspersed with skylights has been hailed for award-winning architectural design.

The Hahn project was at the hub of the 306 acres in Culver City's initial Redevelopment Program. The plan called

Center Court as it looks today.

first for the mall, then condominium housing and commercial office space. (Nearby Corporate Pointe, with 1.5 million square feet of mixed-use commercial and retail space, will grow to 10 buildings.)

In response to increased retail competition in the trade area, Fox Hills Mall underwent an exciting $5.5-million remodeling in 1988 to create a brighter, more contemporary look. Cool tones of mauve and blue enhance interior landscaping that accents new seating areas. The unique clock tower at center court was reconfigured, and a reflecting pool was added at its base.

During the remodel the mall added "Food Fare on 3," which includes 10 restaurants and seating for 350. At the same time a pushcart program was launched to bring in vendors to sell their colorful wares. The program adds

vivacity to the mall and encourages entrepreneurs with small retail businesses to grow into full-fledged merchants with long-term stores in the mall.

A top competitor in serving customers who want convenience, stress-free shopping, good selections in merchandise, and value for their dollar, Fox Hills Mall is an established shopping center that stays on fashion's cutting edge. Through a highly creative advertising campaign, the mall is positioned as the only regional shopping center in the area that reflects a strong multi-ethnic, fashion-forward image. It is an important niche in a city of such diverse cultures and life-styles.

Fox Hills Mall is committed to community activities, and supports many civic groups with a variety of interests. For example, recent mall programs saluted Hispanic culture, gave kids safe Trick or Treating on Halloween, provided thousands of Christmas gifts for foster children, and supported Olympic festivals. An annual art show to celebrate Black History Month regularly attracts crowds of 150,000.

The original mall site.

Spartan Supply Company

Warren Betts once thought he would be a math teacher. Instead, he went to work in a "one-horse lumberyard" in the Imperial Valley and began a long family tradition of service through the building material business. He came to Culver City in 1921 where he entered the lumber business. Over the past seventy years, through many changes, the business has become Spartan Supply Company.

Today Spartan Supply Company's business consists solely of roofing materials for residential and commercial properties.

The firm originally evolved from Betts-Sine Lumber Company which was formed from a partnership with Mrs.

Rick Betts, pictured here at the Spartan Supply Roofing Materials building, continues a long family tradition of quality products combined with customer service.

J.K. Sine in 1934. Soon Warren became sole owner, and when his sons Robert (Bob) and Harrison (Red) came of age, they joined him in 1949. They assumed control of the company when Warren retired in 1968.

The company grew steadily with the area, and in the 1960s purchased Palms Lumber Company (a firm that dated from 1907) and added two other family members, Red's sons Rick and Tom. In 1978 Spartan Supply Company was started on the original Palms Lumber Co. property with Rick Betts as president. Changes in the 1980s were far-reaching: Bob re-

tired, Tom relocated to Seattle, and 1the Betts-Sine lumber portion was discontinued after 54 years. Rick became sole owner of Spartan and it was moved to the Betts-Sine property at the 8770 Washington Boulevard location. Red retired in 1989, though he continues as a consultant.

The Betts family is known in Culver City for its civic leadership. Warren, a founder of the local YMCA, and his offspring have been saluted many times for their ongoing work.

Spartan's large showroom, personal help for the homeowner, contractor referrals, and ability to provide rooftop delivery of materials have made Spartan the major supplier of roofing materials on the Westside of Los Angeles.

The Betts family at the Betts-Sine Lumber Co. (now Spartan Supply Co.), Left to right: Bob Betts, H.F. "Red" Betts, Rick Betts, and Tom

The Rose Family

Since 1948 the Rose family name has been well known in Culver City. First, Fred Rose Upholstery served the community from its Sepulveda Boulevard location for more than 30 years. Now son Steve Rose continues his family's civic involvement as president of the Culver City Chamber of Commerce.

"My parents felt welcomed by America as their new home when they left Germany," Steve Rose notes. "Their business was a way to give something back to the community that made them comfortable."

Fred Rose's given name was Siegfreid Rosenbaum. Like so many immigrants of the day, his name became Americanized. He came over first, to San Francisco in 1938, then his wife Susie followed, fleeing Hitler's regime and World War II.

The Roses and their year-old twin

boys moved to Culver City in 1947; the next year they opened the shop that would serve patrons for 30 years. Fred, the craftsman and salesperson, offered custom furniture; Susie was the administrator.

Steve was interested in his family's business from the time he was "little, up," while his late brother Alan chose to become a pharmacist. (Alan, who died in 1979, married and had two daughters.) As a youngster, Steve rode along with his father on evening sales calls, and often did his homework in the truck.

Steve is a Culver City High graduate of 1964. He attended Santa Monica City College, became an upholstery craftsman, and until 1987 continued in the trade. (Fred died in 1983, and Susie died 14 months later.) Although he was president of the Jaycees, Exchange Club, and oth-

ers, and served on a number of boards (Culver City Family Guidance Clinic, Board of Managers for Culver/Palms YMCA, and more), Rose decided to work for Culver City full-time as president of the Culver City Chamber. He lives with his wife Marlene and their two girls—Dorit and Corinne just four blocks from the office. He has a son, Josh, who lives in Northern California.

Rose doesn't work at his upholstery craft anymore. But he does have his father's tools . . . and a lot of good memories.

Sorrento Italian Market

Although it's called the Sorrento Italian Market, this colorful culinary center has a truly global focus: It features imported "Foods of the World" from South America, Asia, Europe, and the Middle East in addition to its Italian specialties.

Cheerful, with delicious smells filling the air, the store is a treasure trove of good things to eat and drink and handsome accessories for cooking. Its atmosphere makes shopping fun.

"We tell our customers if they want a product they don't see, ask for it and we'll get it," says Albert Vera, who with his wife Ursula established the family business.

to concentrate on the market, he closed the van—goods and all—and kept it as "a sentimental piece."

Albert came to the U.S. at age 15 in 1950 from a small town near Naples, Italy. For a time he worked as a box boy at the Food Palace on Pico, now long gone, learning the business and meeting distributors. He went to Santa Monica City College at age 16, and in 1953 brought his mother and sister to the U.S.

Albert and Ursula met at UCLA while she was looking for a job and he was looking for a typist. "I was having a tough time trying to work and learn English all at once," says Ursula, who

and Albert's mother Lydia in the market. By the late 1960s they had purchased property all the way to the corner to create Vera Plaza—with room to double the market's size (by the late 1970s) and rent space to other tenants.

But all was not smooth sailing. On December 30, 1983, the market was totally gutted by a fire. The Veras say they were able to reopen in two months because people in the community pitched in and helped. During rebuilding, they put in a steam table for hot foods, with all cooking done on the premises for take-home items. They added catering for all occasions, and more recently a ranch in the Central Valley to produce their own fruit, wine, olives, and other fine products under their own label and a Culver City address. (At harvest, as many as 600 workers bring in the crops.)

The business Albert Vera created for his family has also produced a plethora of community goodwill: Numerous sponsorships (for athletic teams, youth groups, and educational and church programs), civic events, and grass-roots political support. In return the Veras have been honored many times for humanitarianism, fair play, and caring about their community.

Sorrento Italian Market.

The market, at 5518 Sepulveda Boulevard, opened November 13, 1962, when Albert Vera decided he wanted a business for his family. (Never mind that he earned a Ph.D. in zoology at UCLA, with an interest in medical research.) The market opened a year after he began a home delivery service, Sorrento-on-Wheels, from a fully equipped van, which he operated for nine more years. When Vera decided

came to the U.S. from Germany in 1956. "I couldn't use my business administration degree because of the language barrier."

The Veras combined their work ethic with family participation, involving their two sons Ralph (now 32, training to be a chef) and Albert, Jr. (now 26, continuing in the business),

"Perhaps the intangible rewards have been the greatest," Albert Vera reflects. "The business has given us an opportunity to have our children around us longer than most. It has given them valuable exposure to Old World traditions. And it has given us a chance to do something for our neighbors and our city."

The Hapsmith Company

Culver Center patrons have been encouraged to take a few things for granted over the years, like convenience, reliability, and familiarity. Those qualities have made the community shopping center a neighborhood staple since just after World War II. Culver Center, anchored by Ralph's Supermarket and Thrifty Drugstore, is a mix of retail and commercial space at its prime 11-acre location between Washington and Venice boulevards at Overland Avenue. Its ongoing success makes it one of most solid performers in The Hapsmith Company's portfolio.

The Hapsmith Company is a pioneer real estate firm based in Beverly Hills. Hapsmith was founded as a partnership between Maurice ("Hap") O. Smith and Frederick M. Nicholas.

Since its inception in 1958 the company has developed and operated more than 10 million square feet of commercial space, including four, one-million-square-foot regional malls, numerous community shopping centers, and several high-rise office buildings. The company has grown to develop and operate shopping centers and office buildings throughout California and Washington valued in excess of $300 million.

Nicholas, now Hapsmith's chairman and chief executive officer, is the man behind Culver Center and all The Hapsmith Company's properties In addition, he is an attorney who has built one of the city's most distinguished professional and philanthropic careers. As chairman of the Museum of Contemporary Art (MOCA) in Los Angeles, he was responsible for developing two museums for that institution. Most recently, he has directed his considerable energy toward chairing the Walt Disney Concert Hall Committee at The Los Angeles Music Center.

Culver Center has

ABOVE: *Walt Disney Concert Hall in Los Angeles, California.*

LEFT: *Culver Center in Culver City, California.*

evolved from its postwar opening through phased changes to meet its patrons' modern-day needs. To continue that process, Culver Center—part of The Hapsmith Company since 1983—will undergo a major expansion and renovation to continue meeting contemporary shopping standards. Emphasis will be on high qual-

International Cultural and Trade Center in Washington, D.C.

ity, yet affordable, goods and services.

Hapsmith's long-term ownership of the center reflects the company's attitude for all its urban properties: to provide goods and services while maintaining a strong community orientation. In that spirit, Culver Center's management promotes serious interest in civic activities through merchant participation and corporate public service. For instance, Culver Center management has offered commercial space to community groups in the interim before redevelopment.

Perhaps the most unique current project for the company is its involvement in the United States International Cultural and Trade Center in Washington, D.C. (under development two blocks from the White House on Pennsylvania Avenue). This 3.1-million-square-foot project, being developed on behalf of the federal government, will include a 2,000 seat concert hall, four theaters, 200,000 square feet of museum-quality exhibit space, 200,000 square feet of retail facilities, and more than 1.5 million square feet of office space for government agencies.

Ramada Hotel

Set in a neighborhood atmosphere with green hills as a backdrop, yet easily accessible from the San Diego Freeway, the high-rise Ramada Hotel combines the best of both worlds: small-town pleasantries with big-city conveniences.

The Ramada Hotel International Airport in Culver City was built in 1974 and extensively renovated in 1986 and again in 1991. A full-service hotel, the property has 260 guest rooms, suites, and executive suites.

"When the hotel was built here, management recognized the potential for continuing growth in the region," notes Ted Ecklund, the general manager. "High tech, aerospace, and retail opportunities with the nearby Fox Hills Mall made this a prime location."

The Ramada Hotel is located at 6333 Bristol Parkway near the San Diego Freeway (I-405) at Sepulveda Boulevard and Centinela Avenue. It is adjacent to the business park known as Corporate Pointe.

The Ramada Hotel International Airport has proved to be especially popular because of its two-mile proximity to Los Angeles International Airport (LAX). It is distant enough to be out of the congestion, yet close enough for convenience. The hotel provides a 24-hour courtesy van to and from LAX.

The Corporate Amenity Program, a high-growth area of the hotel's business, is strong for a number of reasons. The program provides guaranteed corporate rates to member groups, preferred availability on reservations for those registered, upgrades to the best available rooms, and courtesy transportation from hotel to office, along with other advantages.

Understanding the special requirements of women travelers, the hotel offers rooms closest to the elevator and escorts to cars in parking lots on request. Special restaurant seating is also a consideration.

Tourism is well-served with the Fox Hills Mall within walking distance, offering some 138 stores and specialty shops, and nearby Marina del Rey and beach access for visitors. There are special SuperSaver Weekends, a Best Years program for senior citizens, and a Four-for-One offer that draw the nonbusiness crowd to this convenient location.

All classifications of guests appreciate the adjacent park for jogging and tennis, the complete health club with modern equipment and indoor Jacuzzi and the outdoor heated swimming pool in a garden setting, along with the hotel's many other amenities.

The surrounding residential neighborhoods and commercial enterprises in Culver City make good use of the hotel's 10 meeting and banquet rooms and ballroom. Facilities can accommodate up to 300 persons, and arrangements are handled by the hotel's highly professional staff, which is experienced in meeting and food and beverage service planning. Events range from conventions, private board meetings, and training sessions to wedding receptions, birthday parties, and other social events.

Just off the main lobby, the Ramada Hotel International Airport offers its award-winning restaurant, Cafe Fennel. With its marble flooring and wool-blend carpets from England, overstuffed loveseats, mahogany paneling, beveled glass, and rich, soft colors, the restaurant's ambience is as appealing as its menu.

Known to Culver City residents for its Sunday brunch, Cafe Fennel offers gourmet dining with a California flair. The restaurant serves American cuisine and specialties with a regional touch to individuals and to groups. In the evening a pianist provides entertainment in the adjacent Cafe Lounge while guests enjoy their favorite beverages.

Positioned as a mid-priced property, the Ramada Hotel International

Airport nevertheless holds its full-service designation because of its range of amenities: the restaurant serves three meals a day, offers room service, and provides group catering for business sessions.

Staff members bring international backgrounds and multilingual capabilities to their work. They have made their hotel an award-winning property in the Ramada system, with a sec-

ond place "Hotel of the Year" in 1988 and 1989, and an acclaim for guest service in 1990. The hotel was also nominated for Hotel of the Year and Food Service awards in 1991.

The Ramada Hotel International Airport is part of the worldwide Ramada network, which offers more than 600 hotels, Renaissance Hotels, and inns throughout the United States, the Caribbean, Asia, and the Pacific, Canada, Central America, and Europe. They are located on beachfronts, in historic settings, adjacent to theme parks, and convenient to metropolitan areas.

All Ramada properties, of which there are 30 in California, offer the "Ramada Business Card" program that allows visitors to earn points on monies spent during a stay: room, food, even tax counts toward the program that ultimately pays off in favorable rates, free same-room accommodations for spouses, special discounts, and so on.

The Ramada Hotel International Airport offers a unique touch the others can't. Taking civic involvement seriously, the hotel honors the city's screenland history by naming its meeting rooms accordingly: Actors, Writers, Producers, and Directors.

Culver City News

"We take the news events of Culver City and treat them like the *Los Angeles Times* would treat major international stories," says Steve Hadland, president and co-publisher of the *Culver City News*. "From our perspective, if a story doesn't happen in Culver City, it doesn't happen at all."

The *Culver City News* has been giving top priority to community news since it opened for business in the early 1920s, several different names and ownerships ago.

The paper, which got its current moniker in the 1970s, remains Culver City's only home-based newspaper, fulfilling its dual historical purpose of covering local news first and best, and offering a local angle on larger stories and issues.

The *Culver City News* is the flagship newspaper of Coast Media Newspapers, a division of Coast Media, Inc., which also produces directories and serves as a commercial printer. The company is headquartered at 4043 Irving Place in Culver City.

Co-publisher Ken Tanaka.

ABOVE: *Since the 1920s, Culver City has had its own newspaper, the latest of which is the popular* Culver City News. *Seven-year-old Patrick Beymer, of Culver City, peddles copies of the original* Culver City Daily News.

RIGHT: *Co-publisher Stephen Hadland.*

Hadland and his partner Ken Tanaka are co-publishers and co-owners of the firm. They note the paper has had only about four changes of ownership in its long history, before they took over.

Its first name was the *Culver City Daily News*, which early on was owned by a company called Pen and Ink. Ownership next shifted to La Jolla-based Copley Newspapers, corporate owner of the *San Diego Tribune* and other newspapers. In the late '60s Copley sold the Culver City paper and its sister publications to longtime area resident Ed Dean, who had learned the business from his father, owner of the *Inglewood Daily News*.

Two lawyers, Richard Bronner and Bob Payson, (now both deceased) purchased Coast Media Newspapers in June 1979. It was during their tenure that current owners Hadland and Tanaka joined the group.

"I came on board as classified advertising director just a month after the lawyer team took over," Hadland recalls. "And Ken joined the staff about the same time, in the business office. My strength was in sales and Ken's was organizational."

Coast Media published eight newspapers in 1979, and bought four more in 1980. Three of them were in Orange County, where Hadland, a native New Yorker, had grown up. They included the *Newport Ensign, Costa Mesa News,* and *Irvine Today.* By 1986 the company had sold the news group and consolidated to the present six newspapers it holds today.

Their consolidated weekly newspapers cover six communities, with the *Culver City News, Inglewood News, Hawthorne Community News, Lawndale Tribune, Rancho Cheviot Hills News,* and *Westchester News* in their stable.

In the mid-1980s the company began to diversify by adding city recreation magazines, most of them quarterlies. Currently, Coast Media serves 30 municipalities and districts in California and Nevada. The company also works with 15 to 20 small to mid-sized chambers of commerce, providing directories, maps, calendars, and other publications.

Coast Media employs 49 people in Culver City. A sales force in its San Jose office, which opened in 1990, serves as a base for the publication of chamber directories and city magazines in the northern part of the state.

In Culver City, many of Coast Media's employees have been with the company for well over 10 years and are dedicated to covering the city's news accurately and in-depth.

"Maintaining the integrity of the newspaper is synonymous with maintaining the integrity of the city," says *Culver City News* managing editor John Hartmire, whose own history with the paper spans more than two decades. "When the paper was known as the

As with its predecessor, this September 1, 1927 issue of the Culver City Daily News *the* Culver City News *is published "so the people may know. . ."*

The Culver City News is the flagship paper in Coast Media's chain of community newspapers. The papers cover local issues honestly and fairly.

Culver City Star News I used to deliver it on my bicycle."

"We are a reflection of the community," Tanaka says. "The newspaper is a vehicle for Culver City residents to debate local issues. We provide a forum for thought and reflect the mood or temperament of City Hall, of business, and of the people."

Of particular pride to its owners is the paper's timely local election coverage. The *Culver City News,* says Hadland, "has consistently been the first newspaper on the streets with local election results.

The *News* was converted to a tabloid in May 1986 to give readers a modern, easy-to-read format. A substantive weekly, it averages 48 pages, encompassing news, opinion, and letters to the editor, sports, real estate, food, dining and entertainment, public notices, and help wanted and other classified advertising. The newspaper's tone has been characterized by some readers as "scrappy" and "not afraid to fight," yet "honest and fair." The staff has a mission, says Hadland: "to give big issues the play they require, and to provide a community bulletin board."

Coast Media Newspapers have a combined circulation of 70,000, of which the *Culver City News* constitutes 15,000. With a total readership of over 207,000, the newspapers provide a good advertising vehicle for local retailers, political candidates, houses of worship, organizations, and individuals.

Hamilton/Avnet, Inc.

Impressive though it is, the facility at 10950 Washington Boulevard doesn't begin to hint at the size and scope of Avnet, Inc. The company is the world's largest distributor of electronic components and computer products for industrial and military use.

Through broad-based operations, Avnet either ships products as received from suppliers, or offers added value by customizing systems in accordance with customers' requirements. As both reseller and distributor, its primary thrust is as a total solutions producer.

Culver City's "working headquarters" houses Hamilton/Avnet Electronics (product sales only) and Avnet Computer (the total solutions group), as well as several distinct companies-within-the-company that provide in-house services.

The firm's local presence dates from 1957 when Tony Hamilton opened Hamilton Electro Sales, a combination warehouse/distribution center in his garage, and signed his first franchise agreement. Within a year, he moved to a larger spot in Santa Monica and reached over one million dollars in sales. He moved his growing operations again in 1960 to Culver City.

In the same time period, Lester Avnet was building his new company in New York City into a large parent corporation that made or distributed electronic parts, record players, records, and automotive parts. Avnet incorporated in 1956, and in 1970 merged with Hamilton Electro Sales to offer over 60 manufacturer franchises and record sales. Together, the two companies by 1976 had built and opened the Culver City headquarters, Hamilton/Avnet Electronics.

As the industry increased fourfold in the 1970s, so did Hamilton/Avnet grow. Sales and new product lines soared, and key franchises grew as the company solidified its "one-stop supplier" reputation in meeting customers' needs. The company became the undisputed leader in electronic distribution.

The high-energy tone of the industry in the 1980s and 1990s has called for major organizational changes. In 1986 Hamilton/Avnet's computer products distribution was separated from the components operations to better focus on customers' specific needs, forming Avnet Computer. A centralized, consolidated hub system with satellite offices has further strengthened the corporation's place in the market.

More than 8,000 employees worldwide and approximately 1,500 in the sales force nationwide comprise the Avnet network. Among the electronic components distributed are semiconductors, passive components, mass storage, and applied specifications integrated circuits. Avnet Computer offers an endless list of solutions through engineering, testing, screening, kitting, and modifying systems.

Through its Culver City facility, Avnet is actively pursuing Total Quality Management (TQM) for its vast network, with an eye toward achieving the prestigious Malcolm Baldrige Award. By examining every facet of its organization, Avnet's leaders intend to continue as a pacesetter within its employee population, industry, and the community at large.

Patrons

The following individuals, companies, and organizations have made a valuable commitment to the quality of this publication. Windsor Publications and the Culver City Chamber of Commerce gratefully acknowledge their participation in *Culver City: The Heart of Screenland.*

Alliance Bank*
Brotman Medical Center*
Bun's Radiator Sales & Service*
Center Paint & Wallpaper*
Century 21-Dan Cavanaugh Realtors*
The Coombs Family*
Culver City Animal Hospital*
Culver City News*
Culver National Bank*
Culver Park Realty-Dan Patacchia*
The Culver Studios *
Didi Hirsch Community Mental
    Health Center*
Fox Hills Mall*
Hamilton/Avnet, Inc.*
The Hapsmith Company*
Jin's Shell*
The Quirarte Family *
Ramada Hotel*
E.V. Roberts & Associates*
Rolling Greens*
Roll N' Rye Restaurant*
The Rose Family*
Sony Pictures Studios*
Sorrento Italian Market*
Southern California Nursery, Inc.*
Spartan Supply Company*

*Partners in Progress of *Culver City: The Heart of Screenland.* The histories of these companies and organizations appear in Chapter 7, beginning on page 97.

Bibliography

Ainsworth, Ed. *Enchanted Pueblo, Story of the Modern Metropolis around the Plaza de Los Angeles.* Los Angeles: Bank of America, N.T. & S.A., 1959.

Bann, Richard W. "Hal Roach—a Legendary Producer's Beverly Hills Estate." *Architectural Digest* 47, (April 1990).

Bart, Peter. *Fade Out, the Calamitous Final Days of M-G-M.* New York: William Morrow and Company, Inc., 1990.

Bean, Lowell John. "Indians of Southern California." In *Anthropology of the Americas, Masterkey* 59, Nos. 2, 3. Los Angeles: Southwest Museum, 1985.

Beck, Warren A. and Ynez D. Haase. *Historical Atlas of California.* 6th ed. University of Oklahoma, 1988.

Caughey, John and Laree. *California Heritage.* 2nd ed. Los Angeles: Ward Ritchie Press, 1964.

"Citizen, The." Archives with bound editions of *The Citizen Newspaper.* Culver City: The Citizen Publishing Co., 1929-1970.

Coast Media Archives. Microfilm of *Evening Star News,* Culver City News. Culver City: 1950-1970.

Crump, Spencer. *Ride the Big Red Car, the Pacific Electric Story.* 7th ed. Glendale: Trans-Anglo Books, 1988.

Culver City, City of. *2nd Annual Police Benefit Book,* 1927.

———. *3rd Annual Police Benefit Book,* 1928.

———. *Annual Report. 1989.*

———. *1980 U.S. Census Information Packet.* Community Development Department, Planning Division, 1983.

———. *Direction 21, Moving Culver City into the 21st Century.* Steering Committee Report. 1989.

———. Office of the City Clerk: Archives. *Minute/Resolution Books and Microfilm,* 1917-1991.

———. Office of the City Engineer. Archives. 1917-1991.

———. Office of the Fire Department. Archives. 1917-1991.

———. Office of the Police Department. Archives. 1917-1991.

Culver City and Palms Area Directory. Los Angeles: L.A. Directory Co., 1937.

Culver City and Palms Area Directory. Los Angeles: L.A. Directory Co., 1949.

Culver City Chamber of Commerce. *Community Economic Profile, 1990.*

———. *Culver City, California.* Beverly Hills: Windsor Publications, 1963.

Culver City Historical Society. Archives: Research papers on the studios, directories, news clips. 1914-1991.

Culver City Unified School District. *History of Culver City.* Culver City Office of Educational Services, 1965.

Eames, John Douglas. *The M-G-M Story.* Revised edition. New York: Crown Publishers, Inc., 1979.

Fricke, John, Jay Scarfone & William Stillman. *The Wizard of Oz: the Official 50th Anniversary Pictorial History.* New York: Warner Books, 1989.

Goetzmann, William H. "Tying the Nation Together. We Americans." Washington D.C.: National Geographic Society, 1976.

Hill, Laurence L. *La Reina, Los Angeles in Three Centuries.* Los Angeles: Security-First National Bank, 1929.

League of Women Voters of Los Angeles, Culver City Unit. *Conversations with . . .* Los Angeles: October 1984.

———. *This is Culver City.* Los Angeles: March, 1984.

Moratto, Michael J. "The California Culture Area." In *Anthropology of The Americas, Masterkey.* 59. Los Angeles: Southwest Museum, 1985.

Myers, William A. & Ira L. Swett. *Trolleys to the Surf, the Story of the Los Angeles Pacific Railway.* Glendale: Interurbans Publications, Inc., 1976.

Pacific Military Academy. *The Pacific Military Academy Handbook.* Los Angeles: 1928.

Pennington, Lucinda W. and William K. Baxter. *A Past to Remember, the History of Culver City.* Culver City: The City of Culver City, 1976.

"Roach, Hal." *Television and Video Almanac.* 35th ed. New York: Quigley Publishing Co., Inc., 1990.

"Roach, Hal." *The World Encyclopedia of the Film.* New York: World Publishing Times Mirror, 1972.

Roberts, Stephanie. "John Kearney." *The Living Past.* II. Los Angeles: American Profiles, 1979.

———. "Charles Lugo." *The Living Past.* II. Los Angeles: American Profiles, 1979.

Robinson, W.W. *Culver City, California: A Calendar of Events.* Los Angeles: Title Insurance and Trust Co., 1939.

Sadoul, Georges. "Hal Roach." *Dictionary of Film Makers.* Edited and translated by Peter Morris. Berkeley and Los Angeles: University of California Press, 1972.

Smith, Leon. *Following the Comedy Trail.* Los Angeles: Pomegranate Press, Ltd., 1988.

———. *Hollywood Goes on Location.* Los Angeles & London: Pomegranate Press, Ltd., 1988.

Sturtevant, William C. "History of Indian-White Relations." *Handbook of North American Indians.* 4. Washington: Smithsonian Institution, 1988.

Interviews:

Richard W. Bann, 1991; Patricia Culver Battle, 1991; Susan Berg, Culver City Redevelopment Manager, 1990; Gladys Chandler, 1990; Elwin C. "Ted" Cooke, Police Chief, 1991; Pauline C. Dolce, City Clerk, 1991; Virgie Eskridge, 1990; Jody Hall-Esser, Director of Community Development, 1990; Paul and Jo Ann Good, 1990; Alene Houck Johnson, 1990; H. Dale Jones, Chief Administrative Officer, 1991; Syd Kronenthal, Director of Human Services, 1990; Sue McCabe, City Treasurer, 1991; Josephine McMinn, 1990; Fred Machado, 1991; Norman Marback, 1990; Ray and Ramona Moselle, 1990; Paul A. Netzel, 1991; George Newhouse, 1990; Michael Olson, Fire Chief, 1991; Hal Roach, 1991; Arnie Shupack, Sr. V.P. Columbia Studios, 1991; Carmen Shaw Simmons, 1990; Robert Sirchia, V.P. Operations, The Culver Studios, 1991; Pearla Staples, 1990.

Index